LEARNING FROM CHILDREN WHO READ AT AN EARLY AGE

Some children learn to read much more easily than others. However, focus tends to fall on those who fail to read at certain milestone ages, with emphasis placed on diagnosing and solving reading problems. This book explores a different angle – why is it that some children arrive at school able to read fluently?

The book is the result of a three-year research project in which the authors studied a group of children who learnt to read without being taught from before they started school until the end of Year 2, when they were given their first National Curriculum assessments.

By using a study of such children, across a range of literacy skills, as a framework for examining how they make progress during their time in Key Stage 1 the authors produce guidelines which teachers can use to help all children progress with reading.

Rhona Stainthorp is at the Child Development and Learning Group at the Institute of Education and **Diana Hughes** is in the Psychology Department at Royal Holloway College.

D0143899

LEARNING FROM CHILDREN WHO READ AT AN EARLY AGE

Rhona Stainthorp and Diana Hughes

London and New York

First published 1999
by Routledge
11 New Fetter Lane, London EC4P 4EE

Simultaneously published in the USA and Canada
by Routledge
29 West 35th Street, New York, NY 10001

Routledge is an imprint of the Taylor and Francis Group

Typeset in Garamond by
J&L Composition Ltd, Filey, North Yorkshire
Printed and bound in Great Britain by
TJ International Ltd, Padstow, Cornwall

British Library Cataloguing in Publication Data
A catalogue record for this book is available
from the British Library

Library of Congress Cataloguing in Publication Data
Stainthorp, Rhona.
Learning from children who read at an early age/
Rhona Stainthorp and Diana Hughes
p.   cm.
1. Reading readiness.   2. Reading (Early childhood).
3. Language arts (Early childhood).   4. Literacy.
I. Hughes, Diana.   II. Title.
LB1050.43.S83   1999
372.41'4–dc21   98–40353
CIP

ISBN 0–415–17494–5 (hbk)
ISBN 0–415–17495–3 (pbk)

FOR
MALCOLM, MARY AND CATHERINE
ALLAN, ROBERT AND SAM
WITH LOVE

CONTENTS

ILLUSTRATIONS

Tables

Figures

PREFACE

This book has arisen from a longitudinal research project conducted over three years when the children who formed the subjects of the study were in Key Stage 1. We had been fascinated by Margaret Clark's groundbreaking work *Young Fluent Readers*, and were delighted to have the opportunity in this project to revisit her work.

Our work was generously supported by the University of Reading Research Endowment Trust, and we wish to place on record our gratitude to the University and particularly the Department of Education Studies and Management – now part of the School of Education. We received much support and encouragement from all our colleagues.

The parents of the 29 children were unstinting with their time and support, as were the children's teachers. The project would not have been possible without their generous co-operation.

However, the most important people were the 29 children. They have to remain anonymous, but we hope that they enjoyed taking part in the project as much as we enjoyed studying them. We hope that they will continue to experience the happiness and success which they showed during the time they took part in the study.

Finally we must thank our husbands and children. They, above all, know how much fun we had doing this work.

1

IN THE BEGINNING . . .
READING AND WRITING

One of the most important tasks, if not *the* most important task, of the early-years' teacher is to teach children to read and write. Once children are able to read fluently, accurately and independently they have access to a whole universe of ideas that can take them far beyond the confines of the classroom. Once they can write they are able to make concrete their thoughts and so refine and reflect upon them. To be literate is an essential attribute in our society as we enter the twenty-first century. It may be that technology will develop in such a way as to make literacy obsolete, but it is difficult to imagine this happening from our present standpoint: reading is such an efficient means of accessing information and ideas. The skilled reader can take in far more information in a shorter space of time through the eyes than through the ears. The listener is coupled to the speaker but the reader can play fast and loose with the writer; dodging backwards and forwards, re-reading some sections and skipping others. Being able to read and write are essential skills for engagement in a technologically advanced democracy. This highlights just how important the early-years' teacher is. It is her job – and overwhelmingly that teacher is a woman – to ensure that children are taught to read fluently in the first years.

This book is the result of a three-year project which enabled us to study the progress of 29 children from before they started school until the end of Year 2, when they were given their first National Curriculum assessments. Fifteen of the children were able to read fluently before they began school and 14 of them started to read with relative ease once they began to receive instruction in school.

Why study such children? Teachers and students will be well aware that there is a large body of literature concerned with children who have difficulties learning to read, but only a handful of texts about children who learn with ease. One such text is Margaret Clark's *Young Fluent Readers*. In 1976 she published an account of a study of a group of children across Scotland whose teachers reported that they had arrived in school able to read fluently. This was at a time when models of reading development were in their infancy. Since the publication of that seminal work much research has

1

been carried out concerning the development of literacy, focusing not only on developing models of reading development but exploring in depth such metacognitive skills as phonological sensitivity which are now known to underlie reading and writing.

No studies have attempted to replicate Clark's work with the aim of determining how our understanding of literacy skills could be enhanced by examining in detail the development of those children who learn to read without being taught. This book uses a study of such children as a framework for examining how children make progress over their time in Key Stage 1 across a range of literacy skills including reading, spelling, handwriting and punctuation.

Before describing the project itself we provide a framework for contextualising our work. This chapter presents an overview of those contemporary understandings of how literacy develops which have influenced our work.

Language and literacy

One type of task in old 11+ exams – which still occurs in some tests of verbal reasoning – is the analogy task. The children are supplied with one pair of words/concepts which are specifically related to each other. They are then supplied with a second similar pairing of which one is missing, and they have to work out the missing word by analogy with the original pair. For example: HAND is to GLOVE as FOOT is to—? We can make the same sort of analogy between language and literacy: LISTENING is to READING as SPEAKING is to WRITING. The important point about this is that hand and glove are not the same. They have an important relation to each other but are nevertheless distinct. The same is true for listening and reading, speaking and writing. Listening and speaking are aspects of language, but reading and writing are *language-plus*. The *plus* is very important and is the focus of this book.

In the 1970s and 1980s, a very influential idea in education suggested that learning to read was much the same as learning to talk. The obvious inference to be drawn from that statement is that if learning to read is the same as learning to talk, and if children learn to talk without direct instruction, then children should be able to become readers without direct instruction. As we shall argue, the original thesis – learning to read is the same as learning to talk – is essentially mistaken, and therefore the conclusion that children do not need direct instruction in learning to read is built on a false premiss.

Language systems

In order to demonstrate this we need, first, to consider the structure of language. All human languages comprise series of interacting systems. These systems are:

2

- *pragmatics* – language in use
- *semantics* – the meanings structure
- *syntax* – the system for ordering the words into grammatical sequences
- *lexicon* – the words
- *phonology* – the individual sounds of the language.

These sub-systems develop in synchrony, provided that a child has no specific language problems. From the time they are born children are exposed to language. The structure of the brain predisposes them to communicate through the medium of speech. They are eventually able to recognise regularities in the language they hear around them and to derive rules which they then use when they talk. Children clearly use language as a tool for communication; to do so is not something they need to be taught: it is the nature of being human. This is not to say that they would learn to talk and to understand without help. Adults caring for children will make every effort to understand them, and will provide them with many examples of how it is done. They will not be doing this in a structured way, but since it will be happening over a number of years, the children will gradually be able to understand and to communicate effectively.

Examples of how children strive to extract and apply rules when they are acquiring language can be seen in the errors that they make. A very common error in speech production is over extension of a rule. Once children have worked out the rule for making the plural in English they use it generatively and correctly for most nouns. The rule is that if the word ends in a voiced sound then a hard *z* sound is appended to the end as in 'dogs' and 'bananas'. If a word ends in a voiceless sound then a soft *s* sound is added, as in 'boots'. If the word ends in an *s*, a *z* or a *sh* sound then the syllable *iz* is appended as in 'houses', 'mazes', 'brushes'. This is a simple rule which works most of the time, but not all of the time. There are always exceptions to the rule in English. Thus the plural of 'foot' is not 'foots' but 'feet'; and the plural of 'mouse' is not 'mouses' but 'mice'. Yet a very common error made by young children is to talk about 'foots' and 'mouses'. Sometimes they realise that there is something special about these words but they cannot quite work out what it is, so they may talk about 'feets' and 'mices' before they settle on the form which is the 'acceptable' one. An acceptable utterance is one which native English speakers will intuitively recognise.

There is one sub-system of language that turns out to be particularly crucial for developing literacy. We therefore need to elaborate upon it. This is the sub-system of phonology.

Phonology

Phonology is the sound sub-system. All human languages are composed of their own subset of sounds (we acknowledge here that the deaf community uses a language which is based on manual symbols rather than sounds, but does so because of hearing impairment). English has approximately 44 sounds. The actual number that any one person uses depends on the accent and regional dialect. The main sounds of English are given in the appendix, see p. 166.

This list gives the phonetic alphabet which is used to represent the sounds of people's speech regardless of the way the words are written. Throughout the book, when speech sounds are being presented we will use the phonetic alphabet and place the signs within slash marks. Thus the word 'hill' in its spoken form might be represented as /hɪl/ if spoken using received pronunciation but would be represented as /ɪʊ/ if spoken with a south-London accent. Because we will be using phonetic translations per-iodically throughout the book, you will need to refer to the list of phonemes and their alphabet characters in the appendix. At the risk of pre-empting ourselves, you will note that the phonetic alphabet is needed because there is no one-to-one correspondence between the speech sounds of English and the alphabet.

When babies first begin to make sounds they experiment with making whatever sounds they can to hear the effect. They gradually begin to model their output on the sounds they hear around them, so that by the time they are about nine months their babblings tend to sound like the language they hear around them. Children born in England surrounded by the sounds of spoken English will babble in English, just as children born in China surrounded by Mandarin will babble in Mandarin, regardless of ethnicity.

Each word is composed of combinations of sounds. These sounds are called *phonemes*. A phoneme is defined as the smallest unit of sound capable of making a difference to meaning. Take a simple word like 'bag'. It is composed of three phonemes: /b/; /æ/; /g/. We know these are different phonemes because if we systematically change each one we get a different word. If we change the /b/ to /r/ we get /r æ g/; change the /æ/ to /ɪ/ to get /bɪg/ and change the /g/ to /k/ to get /b æ k/.

Phonemes can be classified, as in the phonetic alphabet above, into *vowel* sounds and *consonant* sounds. Vowel sounds are open continuous sounds. The larynx is vibrated as the vowel sounds are produced, so vowels are known as *voiced* sounds. Different vowel sounds are produced by changing the round-ing of the lips and varying the position of the tongue. Every English word must have at least one vowel sound. There are approximately 20 vowel sounds in English, but only five vowel letters plus Y; so it can be predicted that there will be more problems in reading and spelling vowels than in consonants.

Consonant sounds are produced by making varied use of the mouth, including lips, teeth and tongue, voice and nose. They differ from vowel sounds in that they are produced with a more constricted vocal tract. Table 1.1 shows a classification of the consonant sounds based on how they are

Table 1.1 Classification of the English consonant sounds

Manner of articulation	Voicing	Place of articulation						
		Bilabial	Labio-dental	Dental	Alveolar	Palato-alveolar	Palatal	Velar
Stop	Voiceless	p			t			k
	Voiced	b			d			g
Fricative	Voiceless		f	θ	s	ʃ		
	Voiced		v	ð	z	ʒ		
Affricate	Voiceless					tʃ		
	Voiced					dʒ		
Nasal	Voiced	m			n			ŋ
Liquid	Voiced				l/r			
Glide	Voiced	w					j	w

produced – *manner*; where they are produced – *place*; and whether or not the *voice* is used.

In terms of *manner*, the 'stop' consonant sounds are produced by completely obstructing the flow of air before producing the sound. The 'fricatives' are produced by only partially obstructing the air flow, so they are more continuous sounds with a slight hiss to them. The 'affricates', of which there are only two in English, can be considered to be made up of a stop followed by a fricative (hence their phonetic-script character). You will see from the table that these three categories of consonant sound are all paired. They are either 'voiced' or 'voiceless'. Sounds which are produced when the vocal cords are vibrating are called voiced, and those which are produced when the vocal cords are open are called voiceless. The remaining nasals, liquids and glides are all voiced sounds. 'Nasal' sounds are those where the air is constricted in the oral cavity but flows out instead from the nose. 'Liquids' and 'glides' are produced with a degree of constriction of the air as it flows out of the mouth.

The *place* where the sound is made is important. The 'bilabial' sounds are produced by bringing both lips together. The 'labio-dental' sounds are produced by placing the top teeth on the bottom lip. The remaining placements include the tongue. The 'dental' sounds are produced by placing the tip of the tongue on the upper teeth. For the 'alveolar' sounds the tip of the tongue is placed on the alveolar ridge, the hard ridge which can be felt behind the top teeth. For 'palato-alveolar' sounds the tongue is placed close to the back of the alveolar ridge. For the single 'palatal' sound the tongue is arched to touch the palate; and, finally, the 'velar' sounds, which are produced by the tongue being arched so that it touches the velum at the back of the mouth. The best way to get a feel for how these sounds are produced is to make them singly in front of a mirror and notice how /p/ and

/b/, which are both bilabial stop sounds, look the same because the only difference between them is whether or not the *voice* is used. There is one consonant which is not included in the table. This is the /h/ sound. Ladefoged (1982) suggests that this is just the voiceless counterpart of the vowel sound that follows it. This classification of /h/ makes it very easy to understand why people are prone to drop their 'aitches' when speaking.

It is important to understand about phonemes, because when words are produced in written form, using an alphabetic system such as English, each phoneme has to be represented by a letter or group of letters.

A feature of spoken English is that it permits consonant clusters within words. A consonant cluster is a number of consonant sounds which are produced without any vowel sounds between them: e.g. /k l æ p/ has got the cluster /kl/ at the beginning. In English it is possible to have up to three consonant sounds in a cluster, as in /s p r ɪ n t s/.

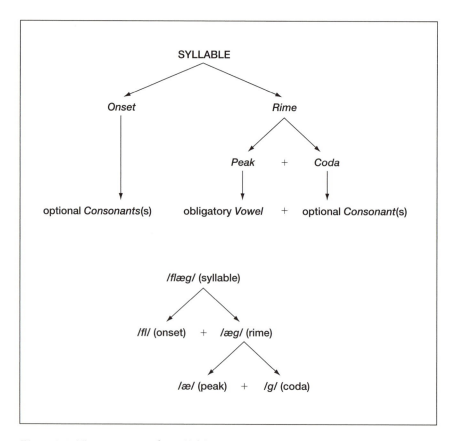

Figure 1.1 The structure of a syllable.

Another significant feature is that English has words which have more than one syllable. A syllable is a sequence of phonemes which contains just one vowel sound. Syllables can be either open or closed. An open syllable ends with a vowel sound: e.g. /p aɪ/; a closed syllable ends with a consonant sound: e.g. /p aɪ k/. The syllable is a unit of phonology larger than the phoneme, which seems to make psychological sense to people. Composers make use of syllables when setting words to music. Indeed the syllable can be considered the 'beat' of the language. Work by Treiman (1988) has alerted us to the importance of the syllable and its composition – the sub-syllabic units of 'onset' and 'rime'. Figure 1.1 shows the relationship between syllable, onset and rime.

The onset is always the consonant sound or consonant cluster sound at the beginning of the syllable, and the rime is the vowel sound plus any consonant sounds that follow it. When people make verbal plays on rhymes they are making use of their knowledge of the sub-syllabic structure of the language. This may be implicit or explicit knowledge and it is possible to be sensitive to rhyme even if one is unable to read.

We have presented a description of the units of the phonological system because contemporary research suggests that a degree of sensitivity to phonemes and rhyme is necessary for cracking the system when learning to read. Teachers therefore need to have a professional understanding of how the system works so that they can make informed decisions about teaching strategies.

Written language systems

The written word is clearly based on the spoken word. It would be foolish to suggest that there is no relationship between the two. However, while there is a genetic imperative for developing language, there is no such imperative for developing literacy. Given a different historical time and geographical location, literacy might not be an option open to us. However, there is in our time a cultural imperative for learning to read and write, and children need to achieve these abilities in order to survive, succeed and, indeed, triumph in our society. There are still large proportions of the different peoples of the world who are not literate, but all those peoples have language. This highlights the cultural nature of this 'manufactured' system.

Writing systems vary in time and place but all were developed to make a permanent visual record of the spoken word. The system used in English is alphabetic, but fairly complex. As the phonetic alphabet in the appendix shows, there are approximately 44 phonemes in English but there are only 26 letters, so there cannot be a simple one-to-one correspondence between letter and sound.

One way in which the system has been adapted to cope with the lack of letters is to make specific combinations of letters – 'digraphs' – stand for single sounds. Thus there is no single letter for the sound /ʃ/, so one way this sound is represented is by the digraph 'sh'. These letters have to be parsed together to represent the sound /ʃ/ and the letters 'ch' are parsed together as a digraph to represent the sound /tʃ/. Because there are at least 20 vowel sounds this procedure has to be used far more when vowels are represented in written words. Some vowel sounds can be classified as *long* sounds and some as *short*. This relates literally to their duration. The /æ/ sound in the word 'mad' is short and usually spelt with the letter 'a'. The /eɪ/ sound in the word 'maid' is a long sound and in this example the vowel digraph 'ai' is used. However, in 'made' the same sound is represented by the letter 'a' and final marker (magic) 'e'. An orthographic device for representing long vowels includes using digraphs made up of two vowel letters, as above, or of a vowel letter plus a consonant letter. Thus the long sound /ɑ:/ is represented by the digraph 'ar' in the word 'cart', though some regional accents words spelt with AR are pronounced with two phonemes /ɑ: r/, and the same phoneme is represented by the digraph 'al' in the word 'half'.

The above example introduces another characteristic of English orthography. Even with the shortage of letters, it would still be possible to have a system whereby every phoneme was always represented by a unique letter or digraph, so that there would always be a regular one-to-one correspondence between them. However, in some instances the same sound may be represented by a number of different letters. For example, the sound /ʃ/ can be represented by the letters 'sh' as in 'shark'; 'ti' as in 'nation'; 's' as in 'sugar'; or 'ch' as in 'champagne'.

On the whole there is less uncertainty about the spelling of consonant sounds, but vowel sounds present a particular problem. The phoneme /eɪ/ is a good example of this. The following words, which is not an exhaustive list, all contain the phoneme /eɪ/, and each time it is represented by a different spelling:

- day   ay
- rain   ai
- rein   ei
- reign   eig
- eight   eigh
- straight   aigh
- bacon   a
- late   a - e
- great   ea
- grey   ey
- champagne   ag - e
- fete   e - e

There are interesting issues arising from this type of orthography which affect reading and spelling in different ways. For example, faced with the written word 'plate', if one knew that the digraph group of letters 'a'+consonant+'e' is almost always represented by the phoneme /eɪ/, then one could pronounce the word correctly. However, because of the many ways of spelling this sound, if one did not know how to spell it, but knew something of the English spelling system, one could hypothesise that it was spelled 'plait', 'pleat', 'plete', 'plaight', 'pleight', etc. All of the misspellings are possible and all could be sounded out as /p l eɪ t/; they just happen to be wrong.

Two of the examples above, 'plait' and 'pleat', highlight another aspect of English orthography. Not only can one sound be spelled in a number of different ways, but in some cases one letter or grapheme can represent more than one sound. The letter 'g' can represent the consonant sound /g/ as in 'goat' or /ʤ / as in 'gin'. Vowels present readers with even greater difficulty. The vowel digraph 'ea' can represent the sound /i: / as in 'seat'; /e/ as in 'bread'; or /eɪ/ as in, 'great'. It can even represent the two sounds /i: æ/ when found in the word 'react'.

When learning to spell we have to learn more than just the possible letter–sound correspondences. There are rules about which spelling of some sounds can occur at the beginning of words and which can occur at the end. The phoneme /ʧ/ can occur in many positions in words: e.g. /ʧ ɪ p/ and /r ɪ ʧ/ spelt as 'chip' and 'rich' In these examples the phoneme is spelled with the digraph 'ch' regardless of whether it occurs at the beginning or the end. Another possible spelling of the phoneme is 'tch' as in 'watch' or 'pitch'. But the letter configuration 'tch' never occurs at the beginning of an English word.

This complexity of English orthography together with aspects of phonology lead to two types of word which can cause problems. English has many sets of words which sound the same but are spelled differently. These are called 'heterographic homophones': e.g. their and there, write and right. There is a particular problem when spelling these words. There are also some pairs of words which are spelled the same but sound different. These are called 'homographic heterophones'. The pronunciation of these words can be disambiguated only in context: e.g. 'the dog's *lead*', but 'the Rev. Green in the library with the *lead* piping'. The *lead* in 'lead piping' is of course also a homophone of *led*. And so we could go on.

The complexity of the writing system is a testament to its history; and it is a testament to human cognitive capacity that the majority of people are able to learn to read and write given the opportunity. However, unlike spoken language, people do not achieve literacy simply by being in a literate environment. The majority of people need to be specifically taught, over a number of years, how to read and how to spell. Since this is the case, when one comes across children who seem to have achieved high levels of literacy without any direct teaching, at an age when it is not expected that they should be reading, one has a unique opportunity to find out what are their particular skills and characteristics.

The reading process

Above we have demonstrated something of the complexity of the English writing system. It is this system which has to be mastered if a child is to be able to read and write with fluency and accuracy. Being able to read and write with fluency and accuracy might be considered a definition of what it is to be literate. Literate adults are those who are able to read almost anything that they choose and write down any ideas they might have so that other literate adults can read them. Reading means that when faced with a text, the reader can work out the meaning. Gough, Juel and Griffith (1992) put forward a 'simple definition' of reading which could be expressed by the equation

$$R = D \times C$$

where R = reading; D = decoding; and C = comprehension.

This is indeed deceptively simple. From this definition a reader must be able to decode the words in the text so that they are accurately translated from visual symbol to phonetics. Also, the reader must understand the text. The mathematics of the definition are important. If decoding skill is at zero, then reading is zero; if comprehension is at zero, then reading too is at zero. Reading at its highest level requires that both decoding and comprehension should be accurate. The chances are that any reader of this book has very high decoding skills and very high comprehension skills, so that reading is automatic and the only limiting factors are interest, the quality of the writing and familiarity with some of the ideas. The readers will not have to focus at the conscious level on the processing of the words themselves, although, of course each word is indeed processed. When skilled readers do skip words these tend to be the short functional words, and they never skip more than one at a time (Just and Carpenter 1987). Comprehension skills are language skills. As we argued earlier, language acquisition is biologically determined.

One very influential model of the reading process, which has been refined and developed over the years since it was first developed by Morton (1968), is called the 'dual-route' model (for a clear exposition of the development of this model see Ellis 1993).

The dual-route suggests that printed words are recognised because they have been seen so many times before that specific identities – called *logogens* – are created (Morton 1968). By this route, called the direct lexical route, words (or lexical items) are recognised as wholes. The route enables the reader to go directly from the printed words to their meanings. Words that the reader knows already have phonological, syntactic and semantic identities. When an orthographic identity is added to these the printed words can be identified more quickly and accurately.

However, the dual-route model suggests that there is another route to word recognition. We know that skilled readers can successfully pronounce words they have never seen before. If this is the case then an argument can be made for there being another route to fluent reading because an unknown written word cannot have an orthographic identity. Obviously, with skilled readers, it is impossible to know whether they have seen obscure words before or not. Psychologists have therefore tested the proposition that it is possible for skilled readers to read totally new words accurately by presenting them with made up strings of letters called 'nonwords'. The likelihood is that you will pronounce *zalinokaton* as /zælɪnɒkætɒn/. The dual-route model suggests that you did this by mapping the letters onto sounds and then constructing a smooth sequence. This means that the item was processed by a sub-lexical route. In this case the resulting phonology does not map onto a lexical identity so the item is verified as a nonword.

There is an assumption that in skilled readers, with fully developed routes, all words are processed by both routes but identified by whichever is the faster.

This model of the reading process is not the only one in existence (see, for example, Seidenberg and McClelland 1989), but it is one that has been built up using empirical evidence generated from the performance of adults and children. It also provides a useful framework for considering the development of literacy. One important implication of the dual-route model is that it assumes that people are able to retain in memory word-specific information in the visual lexicon and knowledge of the alphabet system and its sound mappings.

The development of literacy

When children begin to learn to read they already have considerably developed language skills. At the start of the process of learning to read, their decoding skills are at zero and therefore they cannot read. Learning to decode and then subsequently to automatically recognise a large vocabulary is what learning to read is all about. This is generally what teachers have to get children to learn. Byrne, Fielding-Barnsley and Ashley (1996) have argued cogently that there are some aspects of language that children bring to the reading process and there are other aspects, such as knowledge of the alphabet, that they need to be taught. Good teaching capitalises on established knowledge in order to teach new knowledge and skills.

Ehri (1995, 1997), although not an adherent of the dual-route model, provides a clear description of the four levels of learning to read in an alphabetic system which provides a useful framework for understanding the reading processes that children must acquire.

The four levels are:

1 pre-alphabetic
2 partial alphabetic
3 full alphabetic
4 consolidated alphabetic.

Pre-alphabetic level

All children are at this level of processing before they start learning to read. They understand a great deal about the world around them and they also understand something about school. They may well think that one of the reasons for going to school is to learn to read. Children try to make sense of the world around them, so they may well utilise successful strategies from general life when they are faced with the task of reading. Beginner readers seem to try to remember how to read words by forming connections between the visual attributes of the words they are presented with and the pronunciations or meanings of these words. During their early development they will have constantly been faced with many new visual experiences which they perceive and classify, and so make sense of and remember. They therefore use the same strategy for trying to remember written words. Children will be able to 'read' their environment, so they may recognise the golden arches which form the MacDonald's logo. They may recognise the supermarket signs of Tesco's and Sainsbury's, and brand labels in shops that they have seen at home in the kitchen or on television. They process this environmental print globally, but not wholistically. In other words they store the unique features but not necessarily the detail. Thus they may fail to notice when the name 'Pepsi' is changed to 'Xepsi'. A lovely example of this from a corpus of errors in Scotland is where the child read the word 'ball' as 'yellow', and said 'It's yellow because it's got two sticks in it.' (Seymour and Elder 1986). In the end there are too many words with two sticks in them. This pre-alphabetic stage in reading development cannot be said to be real reading because letter–sound connections are not involved. It is a good start, but it is non-generative, so children at this phase are reliant on experts telling them all the words they do not know.

Partial alphabetic level

Children have attained this second level of processing when they are able to read words by forming partial alphabetic connections between some of the letters in written words and the sounds detected in their pronunciations. At this level children begin to use a decoding strategy. This means that, when faced with a word that they do not recognise, they can use their knowledge of letter–sound correspondences to make a non-random guess at what the word is. This implies, first, that they can recognise the letters and can assign sounds to the letters; and, second, that they are able to hear the sounds in the words. By recognising some of the letters and assigning sounds to them, the child has a means of partially decoding an unknown visual letter-string into a set of phonemes which, when blended together, may lead to a candidate word.

Full alphabetic level

Children can be characterised as having attained the full alphabetic level when they are able to use a complete decoding strategy for new words. They map letters sequentially onto sounds and come up with candidate sequences of sounds which are blended into words. When the new word they are attempting is completely regular, such as 'peg' or has a very common letter pattern such as 'life', then they are likely to come up with the correct word. However, they may use their alphabetic skills effectively and show this by 'regularising' words, such as reading 'pint' to rhyme with 'mint' and 'many' to rhyme with 'Granny'. When reading continuous text they will be able to amend their candidate word in the light of the context. Repeated exposure to the same words in many different contexts will eventually ensure that a permanent record is laid down in what is called the visual lexicon.

Consolidated alphabetic level

As children build up their visual lexicon they become exposed to more and more repeated letter patterns which correspond to the same phoneme blend. This enables them to operate with multi-letter units. This consolidation leads to longer letter patterns becoming part of their knowledge of the language's orthography. The ability to use longer letter units when processing new words reduces the memory load and so enables faster and more efficient reading.

At each level it becomes clear that, as with all skills, the more reading is practised successfully, the better the performance. Stanovich and West (1989) have shown that the amount of exposure to print a child has is instrumental in learning to read. The more a child engages effectively with texts, the more that child will practise the skills necessary to enable reading to become fluent and automatic.

Ehri's description is an attempt to capture the characteristics of children's performance as they develop their skills. She describes the development of word-reading skill in terms of the connections that children have to achieve between the visual word and its neural representation.

Earlier, Frith (1985) had presented a model of children's development of reading and writing which suggested that they developed through a sequence of stages, from logographic – much like Ehri's pre-alphabetic level, through alphabetic to orthographic. In Frith's model reading starts out as the pacemaker, but then writing leads the way as the child grows in awareness of the alphabetic principle. Using the alphabet for writing leads developing readers to begin to use the alphabet to process words for reading. However, as they become sensitive to the patterns of English there is a move from alphabetic to orthographic processing, which begins in reading and then is used for spelling. Frith suggests that reading develops in stages, but Ehri's description of the levels does not imply this. She suggests that, though development at levels 3 and 4 is contingent on development at earlier levels, this is not the case with levels 1 and 2, which are not necessarily sequential.

Stuart (1995) considers the dual-route model a useful one for understanding children's development as well as adult performance. She suggests that the two routes to reading – direct lexical access and sub-lexical decoding – may be considered to develop in parallel.

Developing a truly veridical description of the processes involved in reading is an important scientific enterprise. However, in terms of understanding what and why children need to be taught, all models seem to converge on the need to develop decoding skills based on linking phonological awareness to the alphabet and building up fast and accurate sight vocabulary.

A recent model (Figure 1.2, see opposite) presented by Gombert, Bryant and Warrick (1997) incorporates another cognitive process – that of analogy.

Gombert *et al.* suggest that as children begin to read the visual processing system notices orthographic regularities which happen to be in systematic (though not perfect) co-occurrence with phonological regularities in how the words are pronounced. The cognitive system uses this to allow for the reading of some new words that are neighbours of words that are already known.

It seems to us that reading by analogy could be characterised as evidence of a combination of output from the two routes posited by the dual-route model. Goswami (1991) showed that children could use their knowledge of the word 'beak' to read the unknown word 'peak', using analogy. They would be able to capitalise on the shared rime element – 'eak'. However, in order to read 'peak' correctly they would have to know their letter–sound correspondences to blend the onset and rime into the correct pronunciation.

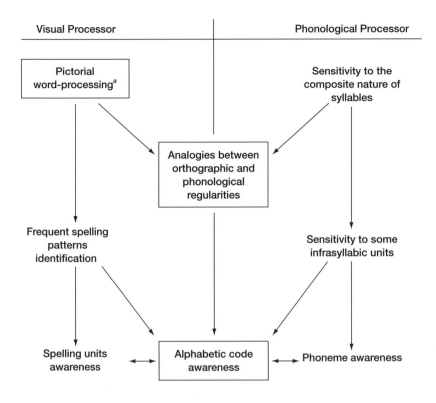

Note:
[a] This pictorial word-processing involves some orthographic patterns

Figure 1.2 The learning to read process.
Source: Gombert, Bryant and Warrick (1997).

Writing

We have already defined literate adults as those who are able to read almost anything that they choose and to write down any ideas they might have so that other literate adults can read them. Just as skilled readers do not have to focus on the processing of the words themselves at the conscious level, so skilled writers do not have to focus on how their message is produced but can concentrate on composition. To quote Ellis: 'If you are writing . . . much of your mental energy is expended on deciding what to say . . . how to express yourself to maximum effect' (Ellis 1993: 59). To be readable, a text not only has to be intelligible to the reader but the form in which it is produced has to be accessible: that is, the writing has to be legible and the spelling has to conform to at least some of the conventions of the writing system in which the reader and writer are operating. If the reader is unable to access the message rapidly and accurately, he/she will be unable to interpret it in the way intended by the writer. Until the skills underlying writing, such as spelling and handwriting, become automatic, much of a writer's processing capacity will be taken up with these aspects rather than with creating the message. Thus: 'To learn to write always involves practice with a tool which has to be brought under control so that the writer can concentrate on putting together the message rather than forming the signs' (Meek 1991: 19).

Graves (1983) described five aspects of the writing process which the writer, both beginner and skilled, has to consider:

1   spelling
2   motor-aesthetic issues – handwriting and layout
3   conventions – punctuation
4   topic and information
5   revision.

Graves believed that it was the first three of these, the 'secretarial' aspects, which become automatic for skilled writers, allowing them to focus on the final two, the 'compositional' aspects. When learning to write, therefore, it would seem important that children gain mastery of these underlying skills as soon as possible. Indeed, Graves found that beginning writers cited spelling and neatness as the most important aspects of a writing task. He believed that their concerns reflected those of the adults with whom they were in contact, and he therefore stressed the need for teachers to respond to content before skills by encouraging invented spelling, and so allowing children to concentrate on composition. However, Graves did not consider the possibility that invented spelling is likely to require more mental energy than does the automatic spelling of the skilled writer, and that the physical act of writing also imposes greater demands on an unskilled than a skilled writer. It is likely that, in the early stages of writing development, emphasis is placed by the writer on acquiring the secretarial aspects of writing.

Spelling

Words can be spelled either by accessing them from the lexicon or, sub-lexically, by segmenting out the sounds that we perceive in a word, applying phoneme/grapheme correspondence rules, and translating the resulting string of graphemes into oral or written spelling. Here we define grapheme as an abstract representation capable of translation into a letter-name or into a written form.

Developmental models of spelling have been largely descriptive. For example, Gentry (1987) described five stages in the development of spelling.

1   precommunicative spelling – the random stringing together of letters, e.g. 'SCheUFc';
2   semiphonetic spelling – the partial representation of the sounds in words. Some, but not all, of the segments in a word are represented by a letter, e.g. 'ra' for ran;
3   phonetic spelling – the representation of all of the sound features of words. There is a systematic mapping of letters to sounds, e.g. 'cach' for catch, 'pla' for play;
4   transitional spelling – the awareness of conventions is apparent and there is an increasing reliance on visual memory. Children, for example, no longer omit vowels or use 'illegal' sound combinations such as *ss* at the beginning of words; and
5   mature spelling – an awareness of basic rules, a mastery of irregular spellings, and the ability to distinguish homonyms are all demonstrated.

Gentry's model seems to imply that spelling in the first three stages is entirely based on the phonemes detected in words, with no influence from orthography.

Frith's integrated model of reading and spelling (Frith 1985), postulated that an alphabetic (phonological) strategy was first developed for spelling, with an orthographic strategy developing first for reading, but with an interrelationship between strategies for both reading and spelling. Further evidence that a phonological strategy is used first for spelling comes from a study by Bryant and Bradley (1980), who found that some young children were able to write words which they were unable to read. The children appeared to be spelling words primarily by using a phonological (alphabetic) strategy and reading words using visual and contextual cues.

Frith's evidence for an orthographic strategy in spelling came from her classification of spelling errors and the extent to which they preserved morphemes or small orthographic units. For example the spelling of the word 'quite' as 'kwight' might indicate that an alphabetic strategy was being used for the first part of the word but an orthographic strategy for the latter part – 'ight' being one representation of /aɪt/, which may be accessed from the orthographic lexicon. This stage is very similar to Ehri's consolidated stage in reading

Recent work by Nunes, Bryant and Bindman (1997) has highlighted the importance of morphological influences on the spelling of some words. The past tense of spoken English regular verbs is formed by adding the phoneme /d/ or /t/ or the syllable /ɪd/ to the end of the verb stem. However, these three suffixes are more usually spelled in exactly the same way, using the letters 'ed' as in 'rained', 'laughed' and 'waited'.

The different ways in which vowel sounds in particular can be spelled has been described above; they also indicate that orthographic/lexical knowledge is necessary if spelling is to become conventional. Spelling using only segmentation and application of phoneme–grapheme correspondences might indeed lead to spellings such as 'plait', 'pleat', 'plete', etc., for 'plate'. It is only once the words are fully represented in the visual lexicon that we know which spelling to use. Lexical knowledge enables us not only to know that the above spellings are not representations of /pleɪt/ but to spell heterographic homophones, for example 'there' and 'their'. This means the lexicon contains information concerning the meaning of the word we are trying to spell. It is important to note that it is not until words are fully represented in the lexicon that spelling errors can be detected. Funnell (1992) argued that it is possible to read words before they are fully represented, but that to produce accurate spellings complete knowledge about letter identities and the positions of letters in words is necessary. This would explain why children may be able to read words but may not be able either to spell them or to identify their errors.

Handwriting

Once a word has been spelled either lexically or sublexically, the graphemes produced have to be translated into some form of motor output, usually by oral spelling, using a keyboard or handwriting. Handwriting is usually viewed as a motor skill but is more properly considered a cognitive skill with specific motor output. For skilled writers graphemes can be realised in at least two different forms or allographs – upper case and lower case. The first stage in translating from the graphemic level to handwriting must therefore be the selection of the appropriate allograph. This selection is dependent not only on both allographs being represented but on the knowledge of the rules governing letter-case usage and on the ability of the writer to differentiate between the letters which represent the graphemes. The sequence of strokes necessary to produce this allograph is then determined, and, finally, the specific motor pathways activated, so that letters appropriate in both size and to the writing surface can be produced. It is necessary to consider that, for some letters, there may be more than one stored sequence of strokes, the form written being dependent on the preceding letter. Taylor (1997) has described two such forms in cursive writing for the letter 'e', one used following 'h, k, t', etc., and one used following 'w, r, o', etc (see Figure 1.3). As with spelling, in skilled writers this process is automatic.

Handwriting has become an area of increasing concern to early-years' teachers now that the National Curriculum includes aspects of handwriting in the level descriptions for Writing (AT3). The current National Curriculum requires that by the end of Key Stage 1 the average seven-year-old is producing letters which are accurately formed and consistent in size (DfE 1995). Because changes take place in the nervous system when new motor patterns are learned, it is important that children learn the correct ways to

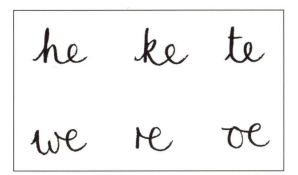

Figure 1.3 The two forms of the hand-written letter 'e'.
Source: Adapted from Taylor (1997).

form letters as soon as possible when they start to write and that they do not
have to change the style of their writing as they move from year to year.
This is particularly pertinent when we consider the introduction of a joined
style, which should develop naturally from individual letters. Sassoon
(1983: 11) stated that 'Flowing, separate letters are quite within the
capabilities of five-year-olds and lead naturally into cursive as the child
matures.' There is, however, some evidence that at least some five-year-olds
do not have the fine motor skills necessary to enable them to form letters
accurately (Laszlo and Bairstow 1983).

Many factors have to be considered when examining the development of
handwriting: pencil hold, the use of lined/unlined paper, spacing between
letters and words, writing speed, the use of exit and entry strokes, as well as
the introduction of a joined script.

Punctuation

Although punctuation is an essential part of writing, its development has
been largely ignored. Hall and Robinson (1996: 1) state that: 'all claims in
articles about teaching punctuation and the demands of the British
National Curriculum documents were predicated upon virtually no
research evidence.' Nevertheless, during Key Stage 1 it is stipulated: 'Pupils
should be taught to punctuate their writing, be consistent in their use of
capital letters, full stops and question marks, and begin to use commas'
(DfE 1995: 9).

Punctuation enables the writer, at least partially, to convey those aspects
of language which are marked by intonation, stress and rhythm in speech.
However, both Read (1983) and Kress (1994) have stated that it is important for children to learn that punctuation does not systematically reflect the
above aspects of speech and that punctuation should be related to the

structure and conventions of written language rather than being viewed as a means merely of translating speech into writing. It has to be recognised that some of the books written for children contain features which attempt to translate speech into writing, such as the use of underlining, exclamation marks, and different styles of letter case and typeface. These are less often used in more formal writing. Because of exposure to such strategies, it is possible that children, in constructing hypotheses concerning punctuation, may use similar punctuation in their early writing.

Compositional aspects

Most authorities would agree that, for the skilled writer, the focus of attention is on the compositional aspects of writing and not on the mechanical/ secretarial skills which they have already acquired and which they use automatically (Ellis 1993; Graves 1983; Meek 1991). In addition to acquiring those secretarial skills which enable them to focus on the content of their writing, it is necessary for children to be taught how to write in different genres. Beard (1994: 99) has stated:

> In considering the process [of writing] we should not lose sight of the different types of writing which children need to undertake to help them to become independent and adaptable writers in subjects across the curriculum and in different contexts in the real world.

The National Curriculum (DfE 1995: 20) stated that by the end of Key Stage 1 (average age: seven years):

> Pupil's writing communicates meaning in both narrative and non-narrative forms, using appropriate and interesting vocabulary, and showing some awareness of the reader. Ideas are developed in a sequence of sentences.

This indicates, that by the age of seven, children should be acquiring awareness of, and using, different types of writing. There has, however, been little research on the actual content of the writing produced by children during Key Stage 1, when they are necessarily having to focus on the secretarial aspects of writing. Little consideration, therefore, has been given to the appropriate stage at which different genres should be introduced. As Scardamalia (1981: 81) has stated:

> For the skilled writer we may suppose that many aspects of writing are automated and that cognitive space-saving strategies make writing possible without inordinate demands on processing capacity. For the beginner writer however, very little is automated.

It is during Key Stage 1 that children begin to acquire some of these space-saving strategies. Indeed, Kinmont (1990) believed that between the ages of four and seven children write so that they can find out about writing. This accorded with Kroll (1981), who proposed that in the earliest phase of writing – preparation – children learned what he termed the basic mechanics of writing. It has to be considered that, particularly for the youngest children in school, these are the aspects that take up most of their processing capacity. Until these skills are automated, there is little processing capacity available for higher order writing skills. This is borne out by the work of Kress (1994) and Perera (1984), who found that the syntactic structures used in children's early writing were less complex than those found in their speech. Although Perera's work was concerned largely with the writing of children older than seven, she did distinguish some of the characteristics of younger writers, describing their texts as often 'muddled and incoherent' as the writer lost his/her train of thought, leading to repetitions, failure of agreement between tenses and inconsistent use of pronouns. Perera believed that this was partly because their handwriting was slow and laborious. Young writers are also described as being more likely to use 'and' rather than other connectives, to use simple active verbs and to use constructions more acceptable in speech.

Although much has been written about the process approach to writing, there has been little consideration of the development of the interrelationship between secretarial and compositional aspects. Our research aimed to address some of these issues.

'Matthew effects' in reading (and writing)

A very influential paper by Stanovich (1986) articulated a situation of which teachers have long been aware. Some children seem to find it easy to learn, and just get better and better, whereas other children find it very difficult, and seem to get worse and worse in comparison. He called these 'Matthew effects', with reference to the Gospel of Matthew in the New Testament: 'Unto everyone that hath shall be given, and he shall have abundance: but from him that hath not shall be taken away even that which he hath' (Matthew 25:29).

Children who find it very difficult to read are put in double jeopardy. They are not able to achieve the thing on which the whole education system seems to be predicated; but, more importantly, they do not have access to the language and ways of thinking which come from being literate. Their self-esteem is diminished. The more difficult they find reading, the less likely they are to attempt to read, and so the further behind they fall and the less likely they are to want to try. Because of these negative 'Matthew effects' it is of vital importance that we ensure that all children are taught to read and write to the best of their ability and, in addition, that we provide help, as early as possible, for those children who look as though they are at risk of failure.

This book is not about these negative 'Matthew effects'. It is about the positive effects of literacy. We wanted to know about the characteristics and educational experiences of children who find it very easy to read. Best teaching practice should celebrate the skills of very good readers. Logically, by the time a child – who was reading fluently before school – has moved into Key Stage 3, there might be no difference in basic reading and writing between her/him and the rest of the class. However, the positive 'Matthew effects' should mean that the child has a rich experience of reading to draw upon which feeds all later learning. Children who read easily at a very early age have potential access to information and ideas by an independent route. They are not dependent on ideas mediated by the teacher or another adult. They should be able to capitalise on this and extend the range of their knowledge and understanding across the wider curriculum. However, being able to read fluently and accurately is only the first step on the road to literacy. This skill needs to be put at the service of accessing a wide range of genres and working on research and study. These higher order reading skills are dependent on already acquired good basic skills, but may well need to be taught specifically.

2

THE PROJECT

Introduction

As we said in Chapter 1, this book has resulted from a research project monitoring the progress of a group of 29 children from before they started school until the end of their time in Key Stage (KS) 1. We wanted to study a group of children who had experienced success in the reading process to see what experiences they had in school, given that they had pre-empted the role of the teachers by achieving fluency before they were given any formal reading instruction. Our first task was therefore to identify children who could already read and subsequently to identify a comparative group of children who were similar in as many respects as possible, but who were not reading fluently before school.

Identifying the children

To quote Mrs Beaton, 'first catch your hare'. We needed to identify reliably a number of children who were not yet in school but were able to read fluently. However, it is one thing to have anecdotal reports of children being fluent readers at a very early age, and quite another to identify such children for a longitudinal research project. Margaret Clark had written to the primary schools in her area to identify children for her original study. This meant that all the children reported to her were acknowledged as fluent readers by experienced teachers, and so she could be very confident that they were likely to fall into her criterion group. We were wanting to identify children before they had begun their formal statutory schooling, and so we had to develop our own criteria about what we would accept as 'reading fluently'.

The research was due to begin in September 1993. We therefore decided that the initial criterion for including any child in the project would be the expected average level of reading performance for children at the end of Key Stage 1. Di Hughes was a Year 2 teacher with experience in administering the Standardised Assessment Tests (SATs) and so was familiar with the

---

UNIVERSITY OF READING
DEPARTMENT OF EDUCATION STUDIES AND MANAGEMENT

YOUNG EARLY READERS

Is your child not yet 5 years of age, but already able to read?

Do you know of such a child?

We are interested to study the characteristics of and to monitor the progress of children who can read before they enter reception classes

We would like to hear from parents, guardians or teachers

Figure 2.1 The flyer.

procedures for assessing seven-year-old children. We felt that reading a story from a quality children's book in their own home would be a suitably non-threatening initial task which would enable us to identify whether or not any candidates were reading fluently. To be included in the study as a fluent reader a child would have to achieve at least level 2 of the Reading SAT. In other words, at the age of four years, or possibly just five years, a child would have to achieve at least the level of reading proficiency expected of the typical seven-year-old child at the end of KS1. The children were therefore expected to be reading at least two years above their chronological age.

The decision was made that the most efficient way to identify any such children would be by advertising for them in the local areas which would be convenient for data collection. The flyer shown as Figure 2.1 was sent to the nursery schools, nursery classes, pre-school playgroups and some libraries in the areas accessible for data collection in both homes and schools. Funding was such that we felt that a group of fifteen early fluent readers and a matching number of children who were not yet fluent readers would be manageable. We just had to hope that the advertisement would lead to sufficient numbers of parents and/or teachers contacting us.

We decided that parents who contacted us would be interviewed, initially over the phone, to gauge whether the child in question appeared to be reading fluently. This meant that they would be able to discuss their child and hear about the research, including the implications of taking part, without having to make a commitment to the project. The parents of any child who seemed a likely candidate for inclusion could then be asked if they would accept a visit from us in order to explain the implications of the project in greater depth. They were asked if they would agree to preliminary assessments being made of their child and if they would agree to be interviewed. At that point we felt that we would be in a position to judge whether the child met our criterion of achieving level 2 on the Reading SAT and that the parents would be in a position to judge whether or not they were prepared to let their child take part in the project. At one level, self-selection may be dubious as a scientific basis; however, it was considered indicative of the parents' interest in the work and that they therefore would be less likely to feel threatened or put upon by the research.

The advertisement worked. Parents rang the University leaving numbers to be contacted for follow-up telephone interviews. In the main we were contacted directly by parents, although some parents contacted us because nursery teachers or playgroup leaders suggested that they should, and some nursery teachers or playgroup leaders themselves made the initial contact.

During the initial telephone interviews the parents were given a brief overview of the intended research programme and then, if they were agree-able, they were asked about the reading behaviour of their child. We were seeking evidence that the child had learned to read through choice and had achieved fluency. Being able to recognise a few words in the environment and repeat the words of a well-loved book were not considered sufficient evidence. This was a very delicate area. Many parents would be justly proud of a four-year-old child who could read road signs and shops' names. The development of an initial visual vocabulary before beginning school is a very useful first step, but it is not an indication of fluency. Being able to read *Bears in the Night* accurately on first encountering it is more likely to be a sign of fluency. We had to be careful that we did not offend them in any way if we decided that their child was not sufficiently advanced in reading to be included in the project.

The parents of those children who appeared to be likely candidates for inclusion in the project were asked if a further interview, with some assessment, could be conducted at home. The assessment took the form of the 1993 Standardised Assessment Test for Reading at KS1, using the listed books and following the guidelines exactly. There were, of course, two differences. The children were asked to read to someone they had only just met, rather than to a teacher with whom they were familiar. However, countering this was the positive factor that this reading would be done at home – not at school, as is the case with SATs – where the children would be likely to feel more relaxed. The Reading SAT for that year required children to read while a running record was taken. This home-reading exercise enabled us to identify those children who were reading fluently within the criteria laid down by the National Curriculum attainment levels. It therefore ensured that we had a best-first-guess at performance and included any child who was achieving level 2. The children were also asked to do the British Picture Vocabulary Scale (Dunn, Dunn, Whetton and Pintilie 1982), so that we had a measure of recognition vocabulary. This standardised text correlates highly with verbal IQ. During this visit the parent – universally the mother – was given the opportunity to discuss the research and its longitudinal nature, and the level of commitment required was explained.

In addition, we asked the parents to fill in a children's author recognition test. Cipielewski and Stanovich (1992) had been working on simple instruments which would be reliable proxy measures for assessing exposure to print. Their rationale was that exposure to print had been identified as an important factor contributing to individual differences in word-reading ability. However, logging actual exposure to print is a time-consuming practice, so any simple measure which correlated highly with more complicated measures was welcomed. They found that author recognition tests were useful for working with adults. They developed lists which were made up of real authors' names and names of other real people who were not authors. The test procedure required people to simply tick the names which they were absolutely certain were those of authors. When the results from such a test were compared with other measures of exposure to print, such as diary records, the author recognition tests were found to be highly reliable. Stainthorp (1994) used this method to develop a UK version of the children's author recognition test (CART) which was used in a longitudinal study of reading development. The test was designed to be used with children. For the present study we decided to give this children's test to the parents. Stainthorp (1997) had found that primary teachers scored higher on the CART than did secondary teachers, presumably because they were exposed to far more children's literature. Our intention was to match each early-reading child with a similar child who was not yet reading. We therefore felt that scores on the CART would prove useful for matching the parents of the fluent readers with the parents of the comparative group of children who had not achieved fluency before they began school.

The parents were told that the results of any standardised reading and spelling assessments that would be given to their child would be made available to them. They were also assured that the anonymity of their child would be safeguarded.

At this first interview, we sought the permission of the parents to contact the headteacher of the school to which their child would be going. One aspect of the research would investigate the teachers' experiences in teaching these children. We therefore needed to be able to interview all the teachers of the children taking part.

The parents of the children identified as fluent readers were sent a questionnaire which would provide us with details about the parents' educational background and employment experience, and the developmental milestones of the child, including any recollections they had about her/ his reading and writing performance.

The parents were given an exercise book in which they were asked to keep an occasional diary of anything that might seem interesting about the development of their son or daughter, particularly with reference to literacy. We did not expect the parents to keep daily accounts of their child's progress, but we hoped that their recounting of events might add to the richness of our research.

Having identified 17 fluent readers, we then had to identify the children who were as closely matched as possible to these readers, but who were not yet able to read fluently at the start of the project. This did not mean that they would have no reading ability at this point, but that they would not have achieved the fluency expected of seven-year-olds. Each of these children would, if possible, be matched in terms of age and sex and score on the British Picture Vocabulary Scale and socio-economic status to his or her fluent-reading partner. We wanted the pairs of children to have had very similar pre-school experiences, preferably in the same nursery school or playgroup and to be going into the same Key Stage 1 class of their first school. This is where the CART scores of the young early-readers' parents were to be used. We argued that the results from the CART would enable us to match, to some degree, the familiarity that the two groups of parents had with children's authors. This would give a proxy measure of the amount of reading that they did with and to their children (Stainthorp 1997).

This level of matching was never going to be perfect. The most important criteria were that the pairs of children would be in the same initial class and should have the same BPVS scores. Beyond these, each pair should be as close as possible on all other factors, with one reading fluently and one having not yet achieved fluency. The schools were extremely helpful in identifying children for inclusion in this second group and were very careful about negotiating initial contacts with parents of possible pairings. They were also remarkably good at picking out children who shared all the characteristics but who were not yet reading fluently. This made the task of setting up the second group considerably easier.

A word here might be appropriate about the labelling of the two groups in this study. Margaret Clark had used the term 'young fluent readers', but we wanted to develop our own term which would pay tribute to her work but which would clearly identify our own project. We initially used the more anonymous terms 'study group' (Group S) and 'control group' (Group C) (Stainthorp and Hughes 1995), but then decided on the terms 'young early reader' (YER) and 'non-early reader' (NER). The label given to the second group had to be chosen very carefully. We did not wish to indicate that they were not reading at all initially, or to give them a label which would be inappropriate once the study had got underway and they had become readers.

The following chapters relate to our study of these two groups of children. There were 15 young early readers in the study for the full three years and they were paired with 14 non-early readers. Two of the young early readers were in the same class, and they had always been paired with just one non-early reader in order to minimise the intrusion into that particular class. We lost two children very early on in the project. One family moved back to Canada and another moved to the south of France. Unfortunately, the research grant did not include money for following these children around the world!

This book has been dedicated to the children, their parents and their teachers, but it is worth reiterating how grateful we are to them. The research was successful because of their very high levels of co-operation and interest.

Profile of the young early readers group and individual family backgrounds

Of the 15 young early readers, 10 were girls and 5 were boys. This conforms to the stereotype of girls as being interested in reading at an earlier age than boys. However, we would not want to make any claims about this. These children were all in the project because of parental and/or teacher report. We cannot generalise from the gender ratio here to the general population.

The profile of their positions in their families is given in Table 2.1. By the time the project was ending this profile had changed slightly due to three new siblings being born. These figures show that two-thirds of the young early readers were first-born children, and the average number of children per family was 2.07 at the start of the project and 2.2 at the end.

At the start of the project each child was living at home with both father and mother. Very sadly one child's father died during the project.

The fathers were all in employment, with the following selection of occupations: six came from a background of electrical engineering, though they were now in mainly managerial positions; three worked in a managerial capacity, but came from a business studies/social science background; two worked in the computer industry; two were accountants; one was a postman; and one was a journalist. All of the fathers had education up to A level; ten

Table 2.1 Family positionings of the young early readers relative to family size

Position in family	Number in family		
	1	2	3
1st	3	7	
2nd		1	2
3rd			2

had at least a first degree; two had an HNC; and one had successfully taken further professional qualifications. The high proportion of fathers coming from an electrical engineering background is interesting, though we could not possibly draw any conclusions about it.

Just under half – seven – of the mothers were not in paid employment; one was working in her home as a child-minder; two were health visitors; one was a clinical psychologist; one was a public relations manager; one was a part-time shop assistant; one was a part-time legal secretary; and one was in the middle of her degree course. Only one of the mothers reported no educational qualifications at all; three had left school after O levels and three had left after A levels; two had trained as nurses and both had gone on to take further nursing qualifications. The remaining six had at least a first degree, and one also had a PhD.

This profile gives a picture of a group of children coming from stable backgrounds with parents who had slightly more advanced educational qualifications and mothers who were more likely to work than did the children studied by Margaret Clark. This is not really surprising since in the intervening twenty years, higher education has been opened up to a greater section of the school-leaving population and an increasing number of women with young children are employed.

Profile of the non-early readers' group and individual family backgrounds

The matching of the non-early readers to the young early readers was made primarily on the basis of their British Picture Vocabulary Score, their age, sex and pre-school experience and their planned first KS1 class. Given those constraints, we also needed to match the children as closely as possible on their family backgrounds. Though we collected information about birth order, this was not one of the factors for which we tried to control. Table 2.2 shows the distribution in their families of the non-early readers.

Just one new sibling was born to this group during the project. The average number of children per family at the start of the project was 2.36,

Table 2.2 Family positionings of the non-early readers relative to family size

Position in family	Number in family			
	1	2	3	4
1st		6		
2nd		4	1	
3rd			2	1

rising to 2.42 by the end. The average family size of the non-early readers was marginally higher than for the young early readers, though for both groups the most frequent number (the mode) of children was two per family. Ten of the young early readers were first-born, compared to only six of the non-early readers.

As with the young early readers, these children were all living at home with both parents at the start of the project. Very sadly, in this group, one of the mothers died.

The fathers were all in paid employment with the following selection of occupations: seven were in managerial jobs, generally coming from a business studies/social science/marketing background; one was a teacher; one was a medical general practitioner; one was a police officer; one was a research pharmacologist; one was an electronics project manager; one was a security consultant; and one worked for a computer company. Electronic engineering did not feature as a significant element in the backgrounds of these fathers. Of the fathers in this group one had left school without any qualifications; one had left after CSEs and one had left after O levels; seven had at least a first degree, one also had a PhD; two had an HND and one had taken professional qualifications.

Half of the mothers of this group were not in paid employment. Of those who were, one was a teacher; one was a radiographer; one was a compliance officer; one was a research pharmacologist; one was a cashier; one was a part-time shop assistant; and one was a part-time technical writer. Of these mothers five had left education at 16; one with CSEs and four with O levels; four had gone on to take further professional qualifications; one had taken nursing qualifications; three had at least a first degree and one had a teaching certificate.

These group profiles show that the two groups were reasonably similar in backgrounds, with caring and stable homes. There was more variation *within* each group than *between* each group. This was to be important for the project. Any difference in the reading performance of the two groups would be unlikely to arise from radical differences in the home circumstances, and more likely to arise from individual characteristics of the children.

Data collection for the project

The aim of the project was to monitor the performance of the children's reading and writing during their time in KS1. To this end we planned to assess their reading, spelling and handwriting at yearly intervals: in Year R (or at home), Year 1 and Year 2; and their compositional writing in Year 1 and Year 2. Their mean age when tested in Year R was 5.0; in Year 1 it was 5.92; and in Year 2 it was 6.92. Their mean ages when compositional writing was assessed were 5.5 and 6.58. For ease of reading we will describe the children as being five-, six- and seven-year-olds for the reading assessments; and 5.5- and 6.5-year-olds for the compositional writing. At the end of the project each child was given a semi-structured interview about his or her attitudes to reading and writing.

In addition to direct data collected from the children, we interviewed the teachers and the parents each year.

In order to make for ease of reading we have given each child a pseudonym. Each of the children in the YER group has been given a name with at least two syllables. Each paired child in the NER group has been given a name with a single syllable. It is possible to identify pairs of children because they have names starting with the same letter. None of the pseudonyms are the real names of any of the children in the study. Where we have made comments which might mean that a child, parent or teacher could be identified, we have simply not used the pseudonym at all. We feel that it is most important that the children, their parents and their teachers should not be identifiable from this book.

3

THE CHILDREN

Introduction

In this chapter we present portraits of the children gained from question-naires given to their parents at the start of the programme. At this stage most of the YERs were four years of age, though some of them were just five. Clearly the parents had agreed that their families would take part in the project, but they had not been planning on this. This means that the amount of information offered by the parents varied considerably. These questionnaires centred round four main areas:

1   the spoken language development of the child;
2   the development of her/his reading and writing;
3   family reading habits; and
4   family writing habits.

Benjamin

Benjamin had been recorded as saying his first few words at 18 months and was described by his mother as having been a quiet baby. However, by 27 months he was talking non-stop and asking lots of 'how' and 'why' ques-tions. His mother described him as having always liked books, and from the age of 18 months he listened to stories being read to him.

Evidence about early reading related very much to knowledge of the alphabet. His mother's interpretation was that he learned this from looking at road signs, playing with ABC blocks, watching *Countdown*, using the Ladybird *ABC* books and from the newspaper. The family clearly drew Benjamin's attention to the naming of letters. His mother recounted how his grandfather used to read the newspaper with Benjamin on his knee from when he was about a one-year-old. He would tell Benjamin the names of the letters and by 15 months he was beginning to point to the correct letters when named, though he could not say their names. By 18 months he knew all the capital letters. He started nursery school at three years and within the first term was given GINN 360 books to read. By the end of that year he had finished GINN level 4 and at the time of the questionnaire had read Oxford Reading Tree (ORT) level 3 and Ladybird *Puddle Lane* books (reading the complete story rather than the 'learn to read' version).

He liked going to the local library and there were family visits with mother and brother every 2–3 weeks when they all borrowed books. In addition his mother reported that she occasionally bought books for herself or the children. She bought magazines which Benjamin used for finding out what was on TV. His father could also be seen reading the magazines, and he occasionally bought the newspapers at the weekend. Both the children had a weekly comic which they read with their mother.

The nursery school which had encouraged his reading habits sent books home which he read with his mother before bedtime and then to himself when he got up in the morning. The mother read to the children every evening and their father also did this when they were on holiday. The father's favourite leisure reading was science fiction, but he was described by his wife as being 'not a very keen reader'. Her favourite reading was crime fiction, cookery books and gardening books.

Benjamin was reported as able to write in a number of genres without any help except for spelling. He wrote captions for pictures and thank-you letters. He made signs for things and wrote on a calendar to plan his activities. He would also copy his mother as she was writing shopping lists. He did the word searches in his comics and, with help, would do the crossword. Both parents did the crossword in their magazines. The amount of writing done in the home by the parents was reported as limited, though they both wrote letters when they were on holiday. Benjamin's mother wrote lists for shopping and for any jobs that she had to do. She also did bookeeping of the accounts of her sports club. His father did the same for his sports club, using both a book and the family computer. He used a computer most of the time for writing at work.

Additional information included family games of Scrabble. They had Junior Scrabble, but Benjamin preferred to play with the side of the board which was like the adult game. He could usually manage to play unaided, and would also make up his own word games. He had access to the family PC. At the time the questionnaire was completed, Benjamin had almost finished a program called *Teddy Fun School* which involved a lot of reading. He would play other games, often getting into the programs on his own. When watching TV he liked to watch the credits to see if anyone had his name, and he would walk around the supermarkets reading the signs.

Clarissa

Clarissa's mother was able to give some very detailed information about the development of her vocabulary. She had recorded Clarissa as having 23 recognisable words at 12 months; 39 at 13 months; 82 at 14 months; 106 at 15 months; 136 at 16 months; and over 200 at 17 months. Vocabulary counts are notoriously unreliable, but these figures serve to show that she was using a lot of language at an early age. She began to use two-word phrases such as 'dirty bottom' and 'milk gone' at the age of 13 months and by 16 months was producing three-word utterances e.g. 'Allan sleep bed'. Examples of her language at 19 months included 'My sock's come off again, Mummy'; 'My nappy's fallen apart'; and 'Look! Big mess there Mummy'.

Clarissa was just 15 months younger than her brother Allan, and so had him as a role model. She copied much of what he did and was involved from the start in his literacy experiences. This meant that she had been exposed to reading activity almost from birth as her mother read stories to Allan. They always had a book at bedtime, and whenever else they asked for a story. At the time the questionnaire was completed, the children used to choose the book at bedtime and would often then take it to re-read. The books were getting increasingly long and with fewer pictures. Clarissa, as a toddler, had enjoyed going to bookshelves and looking through books. She had alphabet jigsaws and flash cards from the Early Learning Centre. Her mother had always encouraged the two children to read their birthday cards and posters, and to write their own names. Once Allan started school Clarissa had seen *1, 2, 3 and Away* and the Letterland materials.

By the age of 16 months she would finish sentences in familiar stories that were being read to her. By 24 months she was able to recognise most of the capital letters and could also recognise the word 'CAT'. At the age of 28 months she was able to play a game which required that she match cards with a three-letter word to cards with the same word plus a picture, and by 36 months she was a competent I-Spy player. When she started nursery school, her teacher reported that she was faster at word games than a lot of the eldest children in the class. By 42 months she could read new three- and four-letter regular words and some longer familiar words. While Clarissa was still in nursery school, her mother felt that she was fascinated by the written word. She would read road signs and single words in books, and she was always asking questions about words and the rules for spelling them. She was particularly interested in the silent 'k' before 'n', and would remember and apply such rules. She could also identify exceptions to rules, such as 'gh' standing for /f/ in 'rough' but not in 'through'. At this time Allan was bringing home *1, 2, 3 and Away* books from school and her mother realised that Clarissa could read them faster than Allan. By 58 months she was effectively fluent. This can be illustrated by an incident when she was reading a book to herself and asked her mother to help her with a word. She was told to work it out for herself, which she did, but her mother realised that the word had been 'harlequin'! At the time the questionnaire was completed she rarely came unstuck, and certainly never needed to have help with the same word twice.

Clarissa's home was full of reading materials. The family used the local library once or twice a month and had done so more frequently before the children had started full-time in nursery and school. Her father was said to be a 'compulsive book buyer'. The house was full of books, and grandparents used to give them to the children as presents when they visited. There were also lots of newspapers in connection with the father's work, and various magazines. The children were reported as preferring to browse through catalogues. They were bought a comic as an occasional treat. Both parents always had a book 'on the go'. The mother's reading would be modern fiction, twentieth-century classics and Picador books, and the father's would be modern fiction, contemporary autobiography and political diaries.

Clarissa was writing from an early age. She was reported to have started writing words 'spontaneously' at 42 months. In nursery school she first copied the teacher's writing and then wrote independently. At home, her mother would write words on cards, cut them out and then ask her to make sentences. There was formal writing at home in the form of friends' birthday cards, gift tags, notes to grandparents, thank-you letters and postcards. She always wrote her name and sometimes a title on her artwork. She would sometimes write lists and enjoyed doing the writing, such as word searches and crosswords, in activity books. Her mother wrote shopping lists (which Clarissa read), letters to the bank, school, etc., and notes to relatives. She would record appointments on a big calendar, do crosswords on holiday and kept a sporadic personal diary. Her father's job involved mainly writing which was generally done using a computer.

There was a computer at home to which the children had controlled access. Clarissa had been given the program *Funschool* when she was 42 months and had managed it quite well. She now had *Funschool 2* which was aimed at 6–8-year-olds and could play all the reading games. The children liked playing Hangman on the computer and her mother had given her the strategy of doing the vowels first so that she understood their importance. They would also do spelling games on long car journeys, such as saying a word starting with the last letter of the previous word.

Clarissa's mother felt that she had benefited greatly from her elder brother who was very articulate, so she had been exposed to conversation from an early age. However, Allan had not been a fluent reader at the start of school.

Desmond

Desmond's mother was unable to comment on his early language development, but he had been exposed to books and reading early on. He was read to every day as a baby and 'loved it', and at the time the questionnaire was completed his father would read him a bedtime story every evening. He was judged to have learned the letters of the alphabet by the age of about 24 months through watching *Sesame Street* and *Countdown* and by doing alphabet jigsaw puzzles. He would read the letters in street signs. The first word he could recognise was 'school', which he would point out in books and on signs. At 30 months his mother bought him the Ladybird scheme books 1–6 and at 36 months he started reading some *Puddle Lane* books. He was encouraged to take his turn when they read books or comics.

Desmond went to the library usually once a month with his mother, though they might go more frequently. He liked getting out *Mr Men* books. His mother said that she rarely bought books except possibly reference books and occasionally books from car-boot sales. However, Desmond was often given books as presents. The family had been buying a daily and a Sunday newspaper up to the time of the questionnaire, but had reduced this to the occasional purchase. However, they did take *New Scientist*, *Which*, *Needlecraft* and *Radio Times* on a regular basis. Desmond was bought the *Thomas the Tank Engine* comic every fortnight and was always asking for more.

His mother said that she always had at least one book by her bed and would read every night, mainly non-fiction. His father was doing an A-level course at the time, so had lots of text books around for studying.

Desmond would do some writing occasionally. He wrote letters to his grandparents and would also 'help' his father to write on the PC. He would be told the letter and have to find the right key to press. The PC was used by the family for writing, with the father using it for A-level work and the mother using it for letter writing. She also reported shopping lists, 'jobs to do' lists, notes, messages and form-filling as writing activities. In addition to his homework, Desmond's father would write shopping lists and the occasional letter.

Florence

Florence said her first words at nine months. By 12 months she was able to match and say 'yellow', 'blue', 'oval' and 'triangle', and at 15 months she was speaking in sentences. When she was 27 months she could recite her phone number and knew her full name and address. Focused exposure to print began at about 4 months when her mother started to read board books to her such as *Where's Spot?* From then on she looked at books and had stories read to her for about an hour a day. Her childminder would also read to her. At one stage her favourite book was Penelope Leach's *Baby and Child* because she liked looking at the pictures. At 18 months she could recite her favourite books by heart and from this time they used to play picture/word lotto. Before she was two years old she was able to pick out words that she knew in texts. Her mother would write words for her on pieces of card and make them into sentences for her.

When she was three years old she was introduced to the Ladybird reading scheme by her grandmother and made rapid progress through the first four levels, and then started reading other books. She would read the back of the newspaper as her parents were reading and any books she could find, such as *Postman Pat* and *Dogger*. When she started going to nursery school they introduced the children to Letterland, but as Florence already knew all her letters, she was bored with the activities. At the time of the questionnaire she would read books to other children in the nursery school as well as reading to her younger sister and to her toys. She was also teaching the other children at nursery to use the computer because she was the only one who could read the instructions.

The family visited the library regularly. They had also belonged to a book club for four years, so got at least a couple of books sent every month. When Florence was born they joined a children's book club. There were also a large number of reference books in the house. Both parents also read the *Daily Mail* and the *Mail on Sunday* as well as magazines both for work and for leisure. Florence bought a comic occasionally. Her mother reported reading about three books a week in addition to texts she might read for work. These books were described as 'trashy historical and general fiction'. Her father read much more slowly but liked science fiction, thrillers and the occasional science book.

Her mother felt that Florence's lack of good physical co-ordination accounted for the fact that before starting nursery school she could spell common words by saying the letters, but would not attempt to write them. Her situation was made worse by having an operation on a broken arm which she could not use for two months. However, a few months before the questionnaire was completed, she had decided that she could write, and she sat down and wrote the full alphabet. She was beginning to write sentences and her own birthday cards to relatives and friends. There were magnetic letters at home which she used for making words and she would copy other people's writing. Her mother described herself as an 'avid list-maker', and this had clearly rubbed off on Florence. She could order words alphabetically by first letter and sort out the post, and she had her own cash register at home. Besides writing lists her mother enjoyed calligraphy and writing thank-you letters. She also used a computer for writing a support-group newsletter and for her own work. Her father said he wrote 'virtually nothing', although he used the computer for spreadsheets and games. Florence had her own computer with games and educational software. The family occasionally played word games like Scrabble, Rumikub and Boggle, and did crosswords.

Gillian

Gillian first said words clearly at six months, and by 12 months was putting sentences together. She was interested in books from an early age. From about three months people in the family would read to her or show her pictures in books, telling her what they were. She used to sit with her great-grandmother looking through magazines and pointing things out. From about 12 months she began to show an interest in books, picking them up, pointing at pictures and saying what they were. She also learnt from watching the TV and videos. She seemed to be very aware of signs on the road and would ask what they were. She could remember what she had been told and would repeat it next time she saw the sign. At the time the questionnaire was completed, her mother felt that she could read anything: letters from school, signs, newspaper headlines and advertisements. She would try to sound out new words and rarely had to be corrected. There was a family PC which Gillian used a lot. She, too, had the *Funschool 2* program which she often used independently.

The family did not use the local library and were not in the habit of buying books. They did buy daily papers and magazines, and Gillian had comics such as *Postman Pat* and *Pingu* which she could read herself. She also read books that she brought home from school. Her mother reported that both she and Gillian's father read the paper and magazine, but not much else.

Gillian would write for fun, mainly names of people and places. She used the PC for writing and her keyboard skills were reported to be very good. Her mother wrote shopping lists, letters to friends and companies, and special-occasion cards. She was also the secretary of the local playgroup, so would take minutes for meetings and write notices of events. The family played Scrabble and both she and her husband did crosswords. Gillian's father had to fill in forms and dockets for his work, and at home he used the computer and wrote notes as reminders.

Henrietta

Henrietta was babbling at six weeks, copying sounds at 12 months and said 'bye-bye' at 15 months. She put words together at 17 months (e.g. 'book drop'), and by 21 months she was producing four-word utterances: e.g. 'Baby get downstairs me' – interpreted as 'I want to get my doll from downstairs'. At 24 months she was speaking clearly, had a large vocabulary and seemed to enjoy learning new words. She was exposed to reading activity print right from the start as her mother read to her older brother Henry. She would be taken to story time at the local library on the odd occasion from when she was 28 months, and this became a regular event when she was a three-year-old. When they walked Henry to school she would look at the road signs and point to the letters she knew. At the time the questionnaire was completed she had her own bookcase full of books and whenever she had nothing else to do she would disappear to her room and read to herself. She also read while having her hair done and when she was on the loo. This avid reading seemed to begin with her recognising the initial letter of her name. When she was 24 months, she started to learn the odd word, and this probably coincided with Henry starting to learn to read in school.

Henrietta's mother seemed to be the one parent who had a direct intention to teach her child to read. She started her on the Don Doman flash cards from *Teach Your Baby to Read*, but did not do very much because Henry was having difficulty learning to read. When Henrietta was 36 months, her mother started to use a series called *Ready to Read*. By the time she was four, her mother had started using the Ladybird *Key Words* reading scheme and she had a recognition sight-vocabulary of 200 words. At the time of the questionnaire Henrietta had a sight-vocabulary of over 1,000 words and had been introduced to Letterland to help with phonics. She was no longer reading the Ladybird scheme books, but taking her own out from the library.

All the family were members of the local library and visited it regularly. They were also members of a children's book club and bought something most months; usually non-fiction books, puzzle and activity books, and the occasional classic fiction. Her parents took a weekly local paper, a weekly religious paper and received newsletters from missionary organisations. Her father got computer magazines at work and bought *Which*, and her eldest brother bought a monthly computer magazine. Henrietta and Henry bought the occasional comic.

In addition to the papers and newsletters, her mother reported reading fiction – mainly 'whodunits and the classics' – irregularly and also books on child development, personal development and cooking. Her father read the Bible. There was a family computer, so the children were able to play a selection of games using simple educational packages.

Henrietta used the computer for writing. When she was four, her mother started to teach her to write using various commercially produced workbooks. She was able to write thank-you letters and sign cards and invitations. She was beginning to know how to spell simple words, and would sound them out before she wrote them. Her mother felt that Letterland had been particularly useful for the vowels. She would always write her name on any picture she drew and would sometimes write a title for it as well, asking for help with the spelling. She particularly enjoyed writing notes for her father.

Her mother wrote letters, cards, invitations, notes, shopping and job lists, kept a diary and wrote a Christmas newsletter. She also sometimes used the computer to write little stories for the younger children, and the occasional poem. The family played Scrabble and did crosswords and word puzzles.

Jeremy

Jeremy's mother did not remember any of his early language development, but since he learned to talk he had been a 'constant chatterbox'. He had been exposed to print from an early age because she always kept baby books inside his pram for him to look at when he was lying down. He had also listened to the stories that she read to his elder brother Charles. At 24 months he was given a cassette recorder with lots of tapes and books to follow. He loved this and still listened to them. He also often chose taped books from the library. By 18 months he was regularly completing alphabet jigsaws, and at 24 months he started to ask questions about words. He showed an interest in the Letterland characters when Charles was learning to read, but his mother felt that he had picked up reading at about 30 months without sounding out the letters, although she noticed that he did sound them out when he was spelling. As soon as he was able he would read the details of card and board games.

The family used the local branch library and the library in the nearest big town. Jeremy attended storytime at the local library each week and afterwards would sit in a corner and read books that he had chosen. His mother would often go into book shops, and she remarked that Jeremy and Charles used them as libraries, sitting on the floor and reading the books! A daily paper was delivered and the *Radio Times* came each week, which the children used for checking on the time and day of their favourite programmes. They also bought a children's magazine called *Farthing Wood*.

His mother was in the middle of reading for her degree, so she had no time for leisure reading but read many books as part of her course. His father always had at least one book on the go but definitely did not read science fiction. The elder son Charles read non-fiction and occasionally fiction, but not often by himself, whereas Jeremy enjoyed reading anything and was particularly enjoying *Funnybones* and the *Puddle Lane* books.

The family had recently bought a computer and all four used it. Both parents used it for work and leisure and the two boys used it for writing stories and drawing pictures, and occasionally played games. Jeremy particularly enjoyed playing with the screensavers.

Kathleen

Kathleen was described by her mother as 'very vocal and chatty'. She uttered her first recognisable words at about 13 months, and by 20 months she had started putting two words together. At 24 months she was speaking in three-word sentences and naming and matching colours. By 36 months she was making complex sentences.

By eight months she loved looking at books, so that when she started walking, at 11 months, she would collect books and take them to her parents. From 15 months onwards she had a regular bedtime reading from her mother or her father. She started asking about print at about 20 months, and at 24 months she could recognise and name the upper-case letters. By 36 months she was reading and recognising three-letter and some four-letter words, and would play games with them. She had also begun to match words and pictures. The nursery school that she attended used the Oxford Reading Tree but she received no formal reading tuition at home. However, her home experiences had included alphabet books, rhymes and poems, and playing matching games. At the time the questionnaire was completed she was good at a word game called Pazazz which involves naming things with different letters of the alphabet under different categories.

Kathleen visited the local library every two or three weeks with her mother and younger sister Karen. She loved choosing books for the two of them. The family had a book-club membership and bought books several times a year, usually information books such as encyclopedias and dictionaries, and some work-related books, with the occasional fiction. The *Financial Times* was delivered which the father took to work, and he bought the *Evening Standard* two or three times a week on his way home. At the weekend they took *The Times* and *Sunday Times* which both parents read, along with their work-related journals.

Kathleen's mother read a lot, normally at least 6–8 books every three weeks from the local library. Most of her reading was fiction, including thrillers, historical novels and the classics, but also biographies and some non fiction related to her work. Kathleen's father read newspapers and journals related to his work. He also particularly liked travel books.

From about 24 months Kathleen would copy letters and draw pictures. At the time the questionnaire was completed she liked to add little notes in letters that her mother wrote to relatives. They had recently returned from a holiday and together had made a scrapbook of their adventures. Kathleen had written some short sentences and stuck in pictures and shells. Her mother did most of the family letter, card and invitation writing. She rarely made lists, but did the occasional crossword and word search. The previous year she had been doing a course which required her to write essays and take notes from books. Kathleen's father had to mark papers for a correspondence course which he examined. He would sometimes bring home writing to do from work and also had to write at least once a week for an evening class he was doing. The parents played each other at Boggle and they played Junior Boggle with the children. This family did not have a computer at home.

Leonora

Leonora's mother felt that there had been nothing extraordinary about her language development. She seemed to make steady progress and keep up with her peers. It was felt that the key qualities which led to Leonora's early fluency as a reader were her keenness to learn and her 'powers of concentration'. At 24 months she would work very hard to complete difficult puzzles herself. From 12 months she always had a story read to her at bedtime, but at the time the questionnaire was completed the bedtime story was usually read by Leonora herself. She had many books at home and had been bought the Ladybird *Read Yourself* books. Once she had started going to nursery she would come home with letters and then words on cards which she seemed to recognise after being told just once or twice. At the time the questionnaire was completed she enjoyed surprising her parents by reading headlines or TV titles, and would often pick up her own books and read unsupervised for enjoyment.

The family did not report using the local library. They belonged to a book club from which they bought books mainly for the children. Her father was said to love books and 'would rather spend an hour in a book shop than any other type'. The *Independent* was delivered daily and was reported to be the main reading of both parents. Leonora's father felt that he had lost the habit of regular reading and rarely had the time to read for pleasure.

At the time the questionnaire was completed, Leonora enjoyed writing the names of people on paper and cutting them out. She had started to give her drawings short titles such as 'Duck on a Pond'. She had also started to draw pictures about a book she was reading. Her mother tried to get the two of them to write a short diary each day about special events, but they did not always manage to do this. Leonora would say what she wanted to record, her mother would write it out and then Leonora would copy it.

There was a computer in the home which her father used for work and occasionally for writing letters.

Malcolm

Malcolm was recorded as cooing and gurgling constantly at three months and liked people copying the sounds he made. At nine months he was using recognisable words, and would sit still listening if his mother spoke to him. By 15 months he was putting words together and thereafter made rapid progress. By 24 months he loved word games such as rhymes, opposites and I-Spy. He also sang the ABC song and nursery rhymes.

Malcolm's mother had read to him from her books as she was breast-feeding him. She also used to sing the nursery rhymes from the borders on the wall in his room, and by 9–10 months he would fill in the last word of each line. He watched *Sesame Street* from about four months, and by nine months his concentration was so good that he would sit and listen to books being read for over an hour at a time. Play was always led by Malcolm's interest, so his mother felt that no formal training was taking place. She noticed that he memorised books as they were read to him and then repeated them back as though he was telling a story. By 24 months he knew the names and sounds of all the letters, even though his mother was not familiar with phonics at the time. There were magnetic letters on the fridge and he used to 'sell' them to people. When he was 36 months he was given Ladybird *Learn to Read, Write and Count* which he read avidly. He started nursery at that time: Letterland was being used but was not much use to him because he could already read. At 42 months he read and attempted, with 80 per cent accuracy, all the station names on a train journey, and at 48 months he was able to read the verses and messages in all his birthday cards. His mother said that he had an extremely good memory which she felt was the key to his grasp of letter sounds and pronunciation. He quickly grasped the rules of word formation, but just as easily remembered all the exceptions and unusual spellings.

The family used the local library and got some of their reading-matter from there. There were lots of books in the home – children's, adult's and reference. They had joined a children's book club when Malcolm was 12 months, and at the time the questionnaire was completed he was able to look through the club magazine to choose books. They ordered approximately four a year from the 5–9-year-old section. His favourites were *Winnie the Pooh, Revolting Rhymes* and *Usborne First Thousand Words*. There were regular newspapers in the home and Malcolm read the comics and supplements they included for children. He also had the *Sesame Street* comic each month and some puzzle books. Malcolm had a bedtime story every night from 24 months and the whole family read together in bed on Sunday mornings.

He had been given an easel when he was 36 months which he used for word play. Whenever he drew a picture he wanted a caption to go with it. His mother considered that his writing and drawing skills were much behind his reading, but at the time the questionnaire was completed he had just developed an interest in writing and was showing the same memory skills for letter formation and spelling as he had done for reading. He was encouraged to sign thank-you letters and to draw pictures on birthday and Christmas cards. When he wrote his own Christmas cards his mother wrote out the longer names for him to copy, though he was able to work out for himself how to spell most names.

Both Malcolm's parents worked from home and used a computer all the time. His mother was involved in writing press releases and publicity materials, as well as writing and editing a newsletter. His father also produced a lot of documents via the computer. Malcolm was able to play on the computer and also on an old typewriter. He did this in a rather unstructured way, but also played educational games on the PC. He played Hangman and had played Junior Scrabble since he was 48 months, but his attention span was short on this. He regularly completed the crossword puzzles and games in his comics and on the back of the cereal packets.

Nadine

Nadine began speaking at 15 months. She always spoke clearly, and people commented on how grown-up her speech was. Soon after starting to speak she began putting words together. She was reported to have always enjoyed books. At 6 months she was looking at cardboard books. She enjoyed watching *Sesame Street* and at 24 months knew her ABC. At about 36–42 months she began asking about the words in books, usually during the bedtime story. She was given some of the Ladybird books, but after six of them they seemed too easy for her. At 48 months she would read words on shop windows, street names and signs, and she used to scan the environment for words to read. At the time the questionnaire was completed her favourite pastime was playing teacher and reading people's names from TV credits. She had become interested in people with 'MP' after their names and reading news reporters' names.

Nadine had two older siblings and the family had membership of the local library, although they only made irregular visits. They took the *Independent on Sunday*, which her father read, and magazines which were read by her mother and siblings. Her mother read every night before going to sleep, but did not read downstairs unless it was completely quiet, which it rarely was. Her father rarely read, but if he did it was Stephen King and music books.

In terms of writing, Nadine used *Learn to Read with Sooty* books, from which she liked to copy writing. She would occasionally help with writing shopping lists and pretended she had homework to do like her older siblings. Her mother wrote occasional letters to relatives and her elder sister was an enthusiastic writer, keeping up a correspondence with a German penfriend and a cousin, as well as writing a daily diary.

From 30 months Nadine was able to play I-Spy and at 42 months she played Scrabble with her Gran. There was no computer in the home.

Phillip

Phillip's mother judged him to be fairly vocal, but his best friends had been more advanced and she had worried about him not putting sentences together. From 12 months he had loved books and doing alphabet jigsaws. He enjoyed watching a video called *Sooty Learns to Read*, but he was obviously past this stage at the time the questionnaire was completed. At

12 months he had learnt the alphabet from being read the *ABC of Cats*. This had the letter names, not the sounds, but he appeared to use them interchangeably. At 24 months he could play Hangman both on paper and on the family PC. He also had his own Word Lotto and other word games. By 36 months he was blending letters like d–o–g to form simple words, which had been helped by reading *Jen the Hen*. His mother had tried giving him the Ladybird reading-scheme books, but he had found them boring. His primary motivation for reading was to play games, but he also used reference books and sometimes read to his younger sister.

Since birth Phillip had regularly visited the library with his mother and (later) his younger sister. The family borrowed the maximum number of books (both new and old favourites), some to read immediately and others to save as bedtime treats. Occasional visits were made to book shops but most books were bought at car-boot and jumble sales and book fairs. Phillip chose and paid for his own books. Phillip's mother was a keen reader, but because of time restrictions tended to read sporadically; she read both fiction and non-fiction and monthly magazines. Phillip's father regularly read the *Evening Standard* and PC magazines, but rarely anything else. Philip was an avid collector of the *Farthing Wood* magazine, particularly enjoying story serialisations and puzzles.

At 36 months Phillip had been enjoying learning to write letters and numbers using an *Usborne Big Book*. Writing was initiated at nursery school where he was introduced to Letterland, which he enjoyed, although he was beyond this stage in terms of his reading. At the time the questionnaire was completed, Phillip was writing lists, treasure hunts, quiz questions and rules for games; with prompting, he wrote notes and letters. He also enjoyed crosswords and word puzzles. Phillip's mother wrote occasional lengthy letters, and diary entries. She also enjoyed all types of word puzzles – crosswords, word searches, anagrams, etc., and regularly made games for the children at work. Prior to Phillip's birth, her work had involved gathering, structuring and disseminating information. Phillip's father rarely wrote at home but he did use the family PC. This had both educational and 'fun' games for the children. Phillip was able to enter information and print.

Rosalind

Rosalind was reported to have babbled normally and to have said, 'gone', her first recognisable word, at 15 months. She put 2–3 words together at 21 months and was never afraid to use 'big' words, usually correctly.

Between 19 months and 22 months (just prior to the birth of her sister) Rosalind and her mother spent a lot of time looking at and reading books. Rosalind also enjoyed an alphabet jigsaw and playing I-Spy using letter sounds. When given a blackboard at 24 months, she wanted to use it to write names; she copied these from cards made by her mother and quickly learned what they said. More words were added at an increasing rate, and Rosalind enjoyed playing games using the words she knew. At 39 months, she started to use activity books concerned with reading, writing and counting. At nursery, at 46 months, she was introduced to the Ladybird *Read with Me* series, which she completed before entering YR. Rosalind's mother reported that she never taught Rosalind the alphabet or did anything specific to associate letters with words. She stated: 'I worked on the principle that alphabet knowledge would follow the reading and in this case it did!'

The family visited the library every 2–3 weeks, Rosalind and her younger sister both choosing books. The parents subscribed to two children's book clubs and tended to buy books sooner than other toys for the children. The children's comics *Playdays* and *Toybox* were also bought. Rosalind's mother read magazines related to child development (she was a childminder) and read a variety of fiction for pleasure, mainly in the evenings. Rosalind's father read *The Times* daily and an electronics magazine, he also enjoyed non-fiction books and travel stories. The children and their mother often had a quiet reading time when they read to themselves, in addition to shared reading times.

Both Rosalind and her sister were encouraged to sign special-occasion cards from an early age. Around the time the questionnaire was completed, Rosalind was enjoying writing a sentence to go with her pictures, composing simple postcard messages and helping with the shopping list. Neither parent reported writing for pleasure: Rosalind's mother wrote letters, cards and notes to friends, and recorded family appointments; her father wrote shopping lists, but used the PC for writing at length. He enjoyed crosswords and was interested in word roots and meanings.

There was a range of children's software for the PC – mostly for older children, but Rosalind and her sister enjoyed simple games such as Letter Snap.

Shelagh

Shelagh's spoken language was said to have been held back because of her shyness, and she was described as developing about five months later than the average.

From 36 months Shelagh participated in reading sessions with her older sister (who had just started school). She enjoyed her sister's books and asked for more to read. Over a two-year period she developed, through her sister, a good reading vocabulary and phonological knowledge, which meant that she could read longer and more difficult 'new' words with little effort. In contrast to her sister at the same age, Shelagh was described as appearing to really want to learn to read. She also enjoyed story tapes and playing word games such as Scrabble.

Shelagh's father made occasional visits to the library for fiction books; he occasionally purchased music magazines and reference material concerned with computer science, and regularly read *Today*. Shelagh's mother read similar material, and also romance and melodrama; she enjoyed crosswords and occasionally read fashion magazines.

There was no information concerning the development of Shelagh's writing. Both parents reported making lists at home. A PC was used for letter-writing and games.

Tamsin

Tamsin had been a vocal baby and at seven months was saying 'Mum-Mum' and 'Dad-Dad'. She was able to point to body parts and to pictures in books at 12 months. Her vocabulary increased noticeably from 13 months, and she was using short sentences by 19 months – 'Big lady[bird] fall down'. By 20 months she was reciting all the nursery rhymes in a nursery-rhyme book. She always loved new words and would ask their meaning.

When Tamsin was a new-born baby, her mother read aloud to her from adult novels, as Tamsin seemed to like the sound of her mother's voice. As soon as she could sit and reach, Tamsin loved to look at books. She was not physically active as a baby, but enjoyed cuddling up for a story. She seemed, at around 20 months, to recognise the letters 'm' and 'o' and by 24 months could recite accurately from books. At 26 months she recognised several words that were featured on a friend's toy, and at 27 months seemed to understand how words were made. She was also able to sing the alphabet song. By 39 months Tamsin had a large vocabulary of words she could read, and her mother bought her the Ladybird *Tom and Kate Read with Me* books. These seemed to give her confidence and made her more willing to try other, less-familiar, books which she read with ease. Tamsin was described at this stage as seeming to recognise whole words rather than working words out from their sounds.

Prior to starting school Tamsin and her mother visited the library every three weeks. Following her entry to YR, Tamsin's mother chose library books for Tamsin. From the time she was a few months old and showing her love of books, they were bought for her on most shopping trips. Tamsin and her mother enjoyed sharing Roald Dahl's books and the *Farthing Wood* magazine (Tamsin spent a long time reading back-issues). At the time the questionnaire was completed Tamsin had started YR. She always chose one of her 'vast library' of books and had a quiet read on returning home from school. She continued to have a bedtime story, but these were usually short complete stories as Tamsin did not like longer books to be interrupted! Tamsin's father bought a daily paper and the *Sunday Times* – all the family read over breakfast on Sundays. Tamsin's mother also read autobiographies and authors such as James Michener and Paul Theroux.

Tamsin never showed the enthusiasm for writing that she had for reading. At the time the questionnaire was completed she had just enjoyed making birthday invitations and typing 'silly stories' on her Texas Instruments 'Computer Fun'; she had become more enthusiastic about writing after starting YR. She also used magnetic letters to write messages. Tamsin's mother used a PC for writing up minutes of meetings and stories for Tamsin, she also wrote shopping lists and intermittently kept a diary for Tamsin.

Bob

Bob was described as having been a very vocal baby. At 11 months he was saying single words, and his mother felt he was 'storing them up', so that when he started to talk he was putting small sentences together. At 24 months he was speaking very clearly.

He had his first book at about two months, and since then had been surrounded by books. At 18 months he was able to listen to a short story, and at 24 months he would have several stories at bedtime and make comments on what was happening in them. At the time of the questionnaire he had been watching *Playdays* on TV for a year or so, and enjoyed it. By the age of 36 months he could recognise his own name and had learnt to say the alphabet 'parrot fashion'. He had always been interested in numbers and learned to count quite early on. In addition to the stories which his father read to him each night, from 40 months he would then listen to a story on a cassette and follow along with the accompanying storybook. His mother reported that he would generally go to sleep listening to the tape.

The family made irregular visits to the library, generally for children's books. Bob's mother liked reading Jilly Cooper and she would buy magazines. His father liked Stephen King, Wilbur Smith and James Herbert. He also read a number of textbooks and coursework books for the part-time degree (MA) he was doing.

There was little information given about Bob's writing, though he would have seen his parents engaged in such activity. His mother kept a diary, wrote shopping lists and letters to friends. His father wrote his assignments using the family PC and occasionally did the *The Times*' crossword.

Clare

Clare said her first recognisable words at seven months – 'no' and 'Dad'. By ten months she was putting two words together. Her mother felt that she spoke quite clearly but had only been very vocal when she wanted something.

She had been exposed to books from birth. Her mother had put picture books in her pram so there was always something to look at. From when she was a few months' old she would sit on her mother's lap while she was reading stories to her elder brother, and from about six months her mother 'shared real books' with her. Clare had always had her own bookcase, which was full of books that she could reach. She had always appeared to be interested in books, so that they were one of her main choices of activity. She would look at them before going to sleep, when waking up, in the car, and when she was being quiet; she would share them when friends came to play. When she was at nursery school she would watch *Playschool* and *Sesame Street*, but at the time the questionnaire was completed, she had started school and was not particularly interested in TV.

From 24 months she was able to recognise her name by the first three letters. The school used *1, 2, 3 and Away* and *The Pirates*, which her mother felt were not very stimulating. As she was a teacher she supplemented these with sets of books from her own school, including ORT and GINN, though she took care to keep in line with the school level. The school had also used Letterland for a short time, which Clare had enjoyed and which reinforced her letter knowledge.

The family visited the local library every 2–3 weeks and weekly in the school holidays. They all bought a lot of books. They would make weekly visits to the local book shop and buy second-hand books from car-boot sales, fairs and bazaars. They also belonged to a children's book club. They did not take a regular newspaper, except in the holidays, but they occasionally bought the *Times Educational Supplement*, and Clare's mother bought two monthly magazines related to the home. The children did not have a regular comic, but were bought one when they went on a journey. Both parents were avid readers, reading every night and during the day when on holiday. Besides required reading for work, Clare's mother liked P. D. James and 'whodunits' generally. Her father liked Swift, Colin Dexter and Neil Ascherson.

When Clare was 48 months she was able to write her own name (her real name is quite long). At the time of the questionnaire she could write her own cards and birthday invitations and, like the rest of the family, she would make lists. Both parents were required to write at home for their respective jobs, and so at the weekends they would have a time when they would all write together. Clare's elder brother had homework from school, and these sessions helped him to concentrate. Clare liked to be included in this group.

The family enjoyed playing games such as Scrabble, I-Spy, Give Us a Clue, letter dice, word searches and description games. They did not have a PC at home, but everyone used them at work and school.

Don

Don said his first word, 'car', at about ten months and at 12 months he had a vocabulary of ten words. By 18 months he was producing 3–4 word utterances, and was described as being 'always very talkative'. When he was a few months of age, he would sit with his sisters while his mother was reading stories to them, and there were always lots of children's books around. She began reading Ladybird books to him before he was a year old, and at the time of the questionnaire he still had a story read to him almost every evening. From 24 months he watched *Sesame Street* and *Playdays*, and he could do alphabet jigsaw puzzles when he was at playgroup at 36 months. He first became interested in reading for himself when he was 50 months and at nursery school. He would memorise simple books, but he was not actually reading the words. He could recognise some of the letters.

Don's mother took the children to the local library every week and he had been choosing his own books from about 30 months. They bought books infrequently, going to book shops about 2–3 times a year, but had joined a children's book club for Don's elder sister. They did not have a paper delivered, but his father read *The Times* most days in the local library and his mother took a couple of home magazines. She always read a novel, maybe Agatha Christie or Wilbur Smith, 'very slowly' at work during her lunch time. His father used a specialist medical library and read professional journals everyday. He also read the Bible or a religious book every day, as well as reference books, and was described as 'a compulsive reader'. He read fiction only on holiday. He liked light reading, such as books by James Herriot and Wilbur Smith.

Don had started to do 'pretend' writing at 36 months, and at 48 months he could write his own name. At the time of the questionnaire he was writing his name on everything he drew and his mother judged that he drew far more than he wrote or read. She wrote shopping lists and family organisation lists. She would also write letters during her lunch break. His father wrote a prayer journal 3–4 times a week and a family letter on the computer each month. He also used the computer for research, but mainly used a dictaphone for work-related 'writing'. Both Don's sisters wrote a diary for school and letters to friends. Their paternal Grandmother wrote books and travel articles for magazines.

There was a family PC which the children sometimes used. They particularly liked the graphics programs.

Fred

Fred's mother considered that he was not a very vocal child. He had at least two words when he was nine months and by 19 months he was talking in short sentences. He had shown an interest in books from an early age, and from 24 months he had stories read to him. He had a story every night, which might be read in instalments. He also heard lots of nursery rhymes and listened to stories which required him to be involved with the events.

At weekends he would have more stories read to him. He enjoyed the *Thunderbirds* comics, but, as his mother said, they were 'a bit of a pain' for his parents to read aloud.

Since he had been very young the family had made visits to the library, maybe once or twice a month. The children were allowed to choose one book each, and Fred usually chose fiction, though at the time of the questionnaire he had started taking out books on animals. His parents took the *Sunday Times* and bought the occasional comic for the children.

Fred's mother wrote shopping lists and he would often want to copy them. The children were encouraged to write, or copy, their own cards to people. Fred had done some introductory writing, reading and maths in books which had been bought for him, and he enjoyed doing the activities. He also liked puzzle books and doing dot-to-dot puzzles. There was a family computer which was used for work and leisure. Fred had shown a keen interest in it since he was very young and could confidently play games on it. He also had a child's computer which had cards to insert and colour-coded questions and answers. He was happy to play with this and needed help only with the spelling cards.

Grace

Grace's mother felt that by 18 months she had the 'basics' of language and said that by 30 months it was possible to hold a good conversation with her. From the age of six months she had looked at books and had stories read to her. Grace and her younger sister and their mother were members of book clubs and their father took the *Readers Digest*. At the time the questionnaire was completed, Grace was having books sent home from school for her parents to read to her. She had particularly enjoyed Beatrix Potter stories and *The Wind in the Willows*. Her mother said that she, herself, did not often read, but when she got a good book, such as a Florence Steel, then she 'can't put it down'. She also liked reading wildlife books. Her father liked reading the *Readers Digest* and had a preference for science fiction and oriental stories.

Grace had liked doodling ever since she had been able to hold a pen. At 36 months she could write her name in capital letters and could copy writing. At 48 months she could write the capital letters unaided, and nursery taught her about the lower-case letters. At the time of the questionnaire she still liked to doodle, but could now write words if she was told the letters. She had never been 'forced' into writing, but when provided with a pen and paper she would sit and 'write' for ages. She was very proud of her writing and had always been praised for it, even when it was 'unintelligible'.

Her mother made lists for everything and memory notes of things to do. She wrote all the birthday cards and Christmas cards and enjoyed doing word searches and puzzles. Her father, too, made lists and wrote himself memory notes, and would write draft reports for work on the computer and do plans for projects.

Hope

Hope said her first words at about 16 months; by 19 months she was putting two words together and she was speaking in sentences by 24 months. She was interested in books from an early age and began listening to stories from 18 months, at which time she had alphabet books read to her occasionally. She watched *Sesame Street* and began to pick up the names of some of the letters from it. There were alphabet posters in the house and she was bought *Usbourne First Numbers* workbooks and Ladybird home-learning books. Between 33 and 36 months she began to recognise her name at playgroup.

Hope's mother took the children to the library every 2–3 weeks. Her father would exchange book tokens for books when he received them and bought books as presents for other people. The family took the *Independent* on weekdays and a selection of newspapers on Sundays. In addition, Hope's father bought magazines on angling, gardening and natural history. Her mother liked reading fiction and often took out Virago Modern Classics from the library. She also consulted cookery books frequently. Her father read fiction only on holiday.

At 36 months Hope had been shown how to write her own name, which she quickly learnt to do (apart from the letter 'ɑ' in her real name). She helped her mother write birthday cards. Her mother wrote occasional letters, and lists for shopping and jobs. Her father also wrote similar lists. He kept an allotment vegetable planner/diary and did writing for his work at home. There was a computer which both parents used.

Joe

Joe's mother felt that he was slower to start talking than his two elder brothers had been. He spoke his first words at 12 months and was using short sentences by 30 months. At 48 months he began asking questions about print. He could recognise his own name and play with alphabet jigsaw puzzles. He had learned many of his letter sounds at home from various books and games, but his mother had not used a reading scheme to teach him.

The family made regular visits to the local library. Both Joe's elder brothers preferred adventure fiction, but they would occasionally take out non-fiction books to help them with their school work. Their parents selected non-fiction such as travel, gardening, cooking and hobbies. They took the *Daily Mail* and the *Telegraph* on weekdays and the *Sunday Times* at the weekend. They also bought the occasional woman's magazine, computer magazines and children's football magazines.

Writing by Joe's parents tended to be related to domestic letter-writing, notes and lists, and they did the crosswords and word searches. The older children also wrote their homework. There were family games of Scrabble, Boggle and Hangman. There was a family computer which was used mainly for games.

Lynne

Lynne was described as having been 'a very vocal baby'. She said her first words at 12 months; was judged to be 'talking' at 18 months and could sing Happy Birthday at 20 months. There had been books readily available from birth, including her parents reading to her and pointing out words. She had always liked stories being read to her or 'made up' ones. When her elder sister had started bringing books home from nursery and school she had listened in. At 36 months she had started nursery school and begun to learn her letters, and at 40 months they had introduced her to *1, 2, 3 and Away*. The children had been introduced to books when they were babies and then had progressed to word/colour/number activity books. They had story tapes and videos with accompanying books. The children would always ask what the street signs said and Lynne was interested in their globe and maps.

Lynne's mother reported that they both visited the library and made trips to the local bookshop irregularly. They had the Sunday newspapers delivered and magazines which the children would browse through. They were also bought the occasional comic.

At 48 months Lynne was able to write her own name, and at the time the questionnaire was completed her mother felt that she had begun to 'take off'. She made cards and drawings for friends and with assistance would do the writing in them. She played with *Fun with Letters* and liked Hangman and doing word searches in her comics. She liked doing treasure hunts, following notes on paper. Her elder sister had helped her to hold her pencil and to scribble. At the time the questionnaire was completed she was doing written work, letter and number formation at her nursery school, and had letter formation for homework. Her mother wrote letters, cards and notes and did the occasional crossword. Her father wrote notes for his work and played Hangman with her. There was no computer in the home.

Lynne's mother said that she seemed to be progressing steadily with reading and writing. She judged her to be a very active child who found it difficult to sit and read or write for any length of time: 'We do it little and often.'

Mark

Mark and his elder brother were much quicker in their language development than their peers. His mother said that both boys were 'born walking and talking', He was a Letterland child. There was a frieze on his wall and he often referred to the characters. He watched *Sesame Street* videos from 24 months and would also go and find books to be read to him. His mother felt that his interest in letters had been sparked off by his elder brother, who would reinforce his learning. From 36 months he was able to pick out letters on posters and in words painted on walls or the road.

The house was full of books on many subjects at several levels, so the family did not make many trips to the local library. However, they had found it very useful for Mark's elder brother's homework. They took *The Times* every day. Mark's mother would read to the boys on demand or as a subject came up by way of explanation. They liked Dahl, C. S. Lewis and Letterland stories. She felt that the boys seldom picked up a book to read if they were not asked, whereas her husband was a compulsive reader.

From 36 months Mark's pencil control had been as good as his elder brother's, and after a year he could write his own name, though he found difficulty with the joins. He was in a nursery class at the time the questionnaire was completed and was beginning to write all the time. His mother described them as being a family of poor writers: 'None of us are particularly good at English, but our maths is a credit!' However, she was always writing lists, and worked at home on the computer. She also used the computer for compiling the family budget. His father avoided writing as much as possible and was described by Mark's mother as being 'computer illiterate'. Mark had grown up with the computer and was not overly interested in games on it, though he would play them if other people were involved. He liked educational software which involved counting, adding and matching and typing words flashed on the screen.

His mother felt that Mark might have been able to make progress in reading at an earlier age, but they had not wanted to push him. His elder brother had experienced difficulties and she wanted Mark to avoid similar problems. She ventured the opinion that children who learn quickly can be a problem in a large class.

Kate

Kate was described as having been a very vocal baby, making lots of sounds. She started speaking at 30 months, was quickly using sentences and had a wide vocabulary, though she had understood a lot before then. Her elder sister had shown a similar pattern, though at a slightly earlier age. From birth she had been present when her elder sister listened to stories. She had always had a bedtime story, but did not ask for books to be read at other times. She also had a cassette recorder and liked choosing the tapes she would listen to after her bedtime story. She preferred looking at books on her own. She liked doing jigsaw puzzles and at 48 months could complete a 200-piece puzzle in a number of sittings; she also liked matching and number games. From 57 months she would pretend to read books, but refused any help in actually reading them because she considered that reading was a skill that she would learn in school and not before. At her nursery school they did many pre-reading activities but did not attempt to teach the children to read. They had the complete set of Letterland books at nursery and Kate's own Letterland book was one of her favourites.

The children visited the local library regularly with their mother and also made irregular visits to bookshops. They were members of a book club and would visit the book fairs organised at school. Both parents read the papers up to five times a week, and would read professional journals for work in addition to regularly reading a catholic choice variety of fiction. Because of watching her sister, Kate was aware of the use of a dictionary for finding word meanings and of using encyclopedias and specialist books for factual information.

From 36 months Kate was able to write her own name unaided and to follow dots to write short thank-you letters. At the time the questionnaire was completed she had just started school and was beginning to copy what had been written down, but only slowly. She had enjoyed doing the writing activities in Ladybird, Early Learning Centre and Usbourne First Learning books. She liked to write her own activities on the family calendar.

Both parents wrote a lot for their work and would sometimes do this at home. They both used the family computer for writing, and Kate's elder sister used it for writing stories and preparing talks for school. She also liked to play Scrabble with her mother, but Kate did not enjoy joining in with these games.

Nan

Nan said her first real words at 17 months. Prior to that time she had been babbling to other children. At 24 months her vocabulary was increasing, but her conversations still appeared to be in gibberish. At 30 months she was using 3–4 word utterances and would be frustrated if she was not understood. She was chatting constantly at 36 months, but her mother felt that she was not comprehensible; so at 40 months she was referred to a speech therapist. The advice was that she had a 'slight slur' which would clear up at about 72 months. At 48 months she was using idiomatic expressions that she had picked up, and at 54 months she was talking non-stop to her younger sister.

Nan had been given books at about six months and by 12 months was having a bedtime story every evening. She started to look at books herself at

24 months. At 30 months she was watching *Sesame Street* and able to do jigsaw puzzles. It wasn't until she was 60 months and had started school that she first began to take an interest in reading words.

The family visited the local library every week, and the two girls took out five books between them. They were also given books for birthdays and Christmas by relatives and they would buy them at car-boot sales and jumble sales. Nan's parents took the *Sunday Times* and her mother had magazines given to her. She read non-fiction occasionally and liked reading Catherine Cookson.

Nan started to write her name at nursery school. Her mother then encouraged her by buying Early Learning Centre activity books and Ladybird *Learn to Spell*. She would help to make cards and invitations and would write, by copying, her own thank-you letters. Her mother wrote personal letters and made birthday cards. She also wrote the correspondence for the children's playgroup and the lectures she had to give using a computer for word-processing. She wrote shopping lists and did the occasional crossword or word search. Her father worked from home and used the computer for his writing.

Paul

Paul was not considered to have been a vocal baby but his comprehension was good, and once he started speaking he developed a wide spoken vocabulary. He was always fascinated by books and from six months had lots of old favourites, as well as new books from the library. At 12 months he used to 'read' to himself in his cot. At 36 months he became interested in Letterland which he later used in his nursery group. He liked videos of *Postman Pat* and *Thomas the Tank Engine*, and around the time the questionnaire was completed he was enjoying watching *Sesame Street, Playday* and *Words and Pictures.*

The family made frequent visits to bookshops, buying both adult and children's books; they also belonged to a children's book club. Regular library visits were used to borrow mainly children's books. The *Guardian* and the *Independent on Sunday* were taken regularly and were read mainly by Paul's father, who also read widely (both fiction and non-fiction). Paul's mother stated: 'I seem to read more children's than adult books!' However she, too, read a wide variety of adult fiction and non-fiction. Magazines and comics were bought occasionally. All the family, including Paul's younger brother, were described as enjoying books and reading something on most days.

Paul became interested in drawing and writing at 48 months, and at the time the questionnaire was completed had a great 'passion' for making books. He was also involved in writing cards and invitations, and occasionally did simple word searches and crosswords. Paul's mother described herself as 'a compulsive list-maker'. She also wrote thank-you letters and corresponded with friends overseas. Paul's father used a PC for work and the children used it for play – *Kid Pix* and *Reading Maze* were popular at the time the questionnaire was completed.

Ruth

Ruth was an early talker, saying her first words at five months and putting short sentences together from 12 months. She enjoyed books at an early age and would look at them with her elder brother. At 24 months she recognised her name in print and started to listen to her brother's story tapes.

At the time the questionnaire was completed, she had been wanting to read her brother's reading books from school and so her mother had bought some of the *1, 2, 3 and Away* series. Ruth also enjoyed a Letterland book and a word-puzzle game designed to aid letter recognition and word-building. The family did not go to the library regularly but did belong to a children's book club. Regular daily (the *Sun*) and Sunday *(News of the World* and the *People)* newspapers were bought and the children liked *Mr Men* comics. They were also collecting a series of magazines called *How the Body Works.* Ruth's brother enjoyed books by Enid Blyton and having stories by Jack London read to him by his father. The *Encyclopedia Brittanica* was used regularly.

At the time the questionnaire was completed, Ruth enjoyed copying words from the daily papers and also using writing and drawing activity books from the Early Learning Centre. Both parents kept appointment diaries, and Ruth's mother had recently completed a year at college which had involved writing assignments at home. Ruth's father and brother wrote stories together and both the children and their father used the PC – the former for educational games and writing stories.

Sue

Sue did not say very much until she was 24 months, communicating through her elder sister. Once she started talking she 'seemed to say everything'. She had liked books since she was a baby and always enjoyed listening to stories, especially at bedtime. At the time the questionnaire was completed she was able to recognise her own name and several other words, and had some knowledge of letter sounds.

The family made regular visits to the library where Sue, her sister and younger brother would choose six books each. The local evening paper and weekend national papers were bought regularly. The children occasionally had comics. Neither parent had a great deal of time to spend reading.

At the time the questionnaire was completed, Sue had started to tell her own stories from looking at pictures in books. She was able to write her full name at 55 months and could also write a dozen letters of the alphabet and the numbers 1–10. Sue's mother did all the 'official family letter-writing' and cards and invitations. Her father wrote letters only for work. He produced these on the PC, which was used mainly for work with the children using it occasionally to play games. The children liked to play Hangman and do puzzles, and Sue's sister wrote letters to her friends.

4

READING

Introduction

In this chapter we consider the performance of the children on reading-related tasks. The discussion of models of reading development in Chapter 1 shows the importance of phonology in learning to read. In order to map the letters onto the sounds, children have to become aware of the specific sounds in words and have good alphabetic knowledge. At the start of the study we hypothesised that children who are good readers at a very early age prior to being taught would show much higher levels of phonological skill than children who are similar in vocabulary development but who are not yet able to read. We also predicted that they would have greater alphabetic knowledge. Since reading is more than decoding, we predicted that these children would not just be 'barking at print'. The efficiency of their reading could be expected to have been scaffolded both by their decoding skills *and* by their experiences with print in general. Because of their word-reading ability, their everyday encounters with books would have enabled them to internalise a deep understanding of how print works.

We used the Concepts about Print Test (Clay 1979) to investigate the children's level of knowledge of how print works. We asked them to perform a series of tasks which varied in complexity in order to investigate their phonological abilities. In addition to monitoring their phonological skills we monitored their knowledge of the alphabet: phonology and knowledge of the alphabet being the two factors which seem crucial to reading development. We also gave the children a series of (made up) nonwords to read. When people attempt to read nonwords they have not seen before they have to use their decoding skills to construct a plausible phonological translation of the letters. Nonword reading is taken by many people to be a pure measure of decoding skills, and so is a good way of assessing how well children are able to apply their letter-sound knowledge to reading. In line with Gough's simple definition of reading being the product of decoding and comprehension, we also gave the children two standardised reading tests. The British Ability Scales' (BAS) Word Reading test (Elliot *et al.* 1983) is a graded test which measures the level of word-reading accuracy attained and the Neale Analysis of Reading Ability, or NARA (Neale 1989), is a graded passage-reading test which gives measures of accuracy, speed and comprehension, in context. At the end of the project they were assessed by their teachers for National Curriculum KS1 and given the Standardised Assessment Tests (SATs).

All these assessments were given to the children three times at ages 5, 6 and 7 years. This meant that we could monitor the performance of the YERs but also map the progress that the NERs were making relative to the YERs.

Concepts about print

In order to ensure that the YERs were not just barking at print, but really had advanced fluent reading skills, we needed to assess their ideas of how print works. The way we chose to do this was the Concepts about Print (CAP) Test which had been devised by Marie Clay. This test was developed in New Zealand as part of the battery of assessments used to select children for the Reading Recovery programme in New Zealand and is designed to give formative assessments. These give the teachers benchmarks from which they are able to build when starting the Reading Recovery programme. CAP is not a test of reading *per se*, but is designed to investigate the extent to which children have internalised insights and knowledge about how print works. The test is in the form of a story booklet which the teacher reads to the children individually. There are deliberate mistakes at various points in the text which the child is required to comment on, comments being requested as the text is read. There are 24 questions in total and the child can score one point for each correct answer. The test covers the following items:

1 front of book
2 print (not picture) carries meaning
3 directional rule – begin at top left
4 directional rule – left to right
5 directional rule – down the page
6 word-by-word matching of printed to spoken word
7 first (beginning) and last (end) of text on the page
8 awareness of correct orientation of a picture
9 awareness of the correct orientation of the print
10 awareness of line sequencing
11 awareness that the left page is read before the right page
12 awareness of printed word order not matching spoken word order
13 awareness of a word's incorrect letter order

14 ditto
15 function of a question mark
16 function of a full stop
17 function of a comma
18 function of quotation (speech) marks
19 upper and lower case correspondence
20 awareness of words with same letters in reverse order: e.g. no on
21 concept of 'letter'
22 concept of 'word'
23 concept of first and last letters
24 concept of capital letter.

The teacher always reads the text as if it were correct and then might ask, as in items 12 or 13, if the child notices anything wrong on the page.

Table 4.1 shows the mean scores the two groups achieved on each of the three occasions we tested them. The normalised scores – stanine groups for a 1968 sample of 320 urban New Zealand children aged between five and seven years, as given by Clay (1970) are shown in Table 4.2. The process for converting raw scores to stanines distributes the data according to a normal distribution curve ranging from 1 (lowest) to 9 (highest).

If we compare the YERs with the New Zealand data we see that at the age of five the YERs were scoring at the top of the range given for the New Zealand children across a 2-year age span. The NERs were performing at the average level for the 5–7 year-old New Zealand children, though they were always behind the YERs. It was not until the NERs were aged seven that they achieved the level reached by the YERs at the age of five.

Clay also gives expectations for the ages at which 50 per cent of a

Table 4.1 Mean score for the Concepts about Print Test achieved at ages 5, 6 and 7

	Aged 5	Aged 6	Aged 7
YER	19.4	21.4	22.8
NER	11.9	17.0	20.2

Table 4.2 Normalised scores for the Concepts about Print Test: stanine groups

	Stanine group								
	1	2	3	4	5	6	7	8	9
Test score	0	1–4	5–7	8–11	12–14	15–17	18–20	21–2	23–4

Source: Clay (1970)

Table 4.3 Comparison of Clay's (1970) data for the performance of European children on the CAP Test with the performance of YERs and NERs at ages 5, 6 and 7

Test	Age at which 50% European children pass item	Percentage pass rate NER			YER		
		Age 5	Age 6	Age7	Age 5	Age 6	Age 7
1	5.5	100	100	100	100	100	100
2	5.0	100	100	100	100	100	100
3	5.5	100	100	100	100	100	100
4	5.5	100	100	100	100	100	100
5	5.5	100	100	100	100	100	100
6	5.5	7	71	100	100	100	100
7	5.5	86	100	100	100	100	100
8	5.5	100	100	100	100	100	100
9	5.5	29	100	100	97	100	100
10	5.5	7	29	36	67	80	87
11	5.5	100	100	100	96	100	100
12	6.5	7	29	71	67	87	73
13	6.5	7	29	92	80	100	100
14	7.0	0	21	43	87	100	100
15	6.5	21	50	71	67	80	100
16	7.0	29	62	100	73	93	100
17	7.0	0	0	12	7	33	53
18	7.0	0	0	29	7	7	67
19	6.0	50	86	100	100	100	100
20	6.0	7	71	100	100	100	100
21	5.5	86	100	100	87	93	100
22	6.0	62	92	92	87	93	100
23	6.5	71	92	100	100	100	100
24	6.5	14	62	71	33	87	100

population set of European children will pass particular items from the 24 listed above. Table 4.3 shows her data in comparison with our own. The numbers underlined show those items on which less than 50 per cent from our two groups answered correctly. The data indicate just how advanced, at the very start of the project, both groups were in terms of their concepts about print, as measured by this test.

The questions about punctuation marks are always among the more problematic items, so that, in Y2, seven of the YER children still could not say what the function of a comma was, though they clearly had implicit knowledge from the way they used commas in reading. It is very difficult to define the function of a comma. Clay (1993) comments that the age expectation for answering correctly on items is 'very dependent on the teaching programme and method-emphasis used in a particular school' (Clay 1993: 50). The figures for item 16 in Table 4.3 are interesting in this respect. Clay's age expectation for 50 per cent knowing about full stops is 7.0 years. However, all the children in our sample were able to score for this item in Y2. This is not surprising since full stops are a feature of the level descriptors for writing at level 2. Full stops are a very important feature of teacher's comments in reports, as we show in Chapter 7. These data highlight the 'environmental' factors in much of children's concepts about print.

The information from the parental questionnaires, reported in Chapter 3, suggests that both groups of children had very similar and positive experiences with books. Their environments had been full of experiences which were likely to raise their awareness of print. The parents were very good about reading to their children. We had also paired the children with respect to their pre-school placements, so the two groups would have had very similar literacy experiences outside the home.

Given that the two groups had very positive experiences, we might therefore suggest that the YERs were in some way in a position to make better use of these experiences to gain insights about how to read the words *per se*.

Phonological tasks

Though interest in the phonological abilities related to reading is relatively recent in educational circles, studies of children's phonological abilities have a long history within the field of developmental cognitive psychology. In 1964 Bruce published the results of a study of the ability of children to manipulate sounds in words. The two types of task he gave them concerned deletion and elision. In a deletion task the child hears a spoken word and is asked to say the word that results if it is said without a specified sound: e.g. 'party' without the /iː/ sound results in 'part'. An elision task is more complex. The child hears a word containing a consonant cluster and is asked to say the word that results when the specified sound to be removed is in the middle of the word: e.g. 'snail' without the /n/ sound results in 'sail'. Bruce found that these were not easy tasks for primary school-age children. The 5-year-olds he tested could not do the tasks at all; the mean score for the 6-year-olds was 1.8; but the 8- and 9-year-olds he tested were able to gain reasonable scores (Bruce 1964).

A seminal 1983 article by Bradley and Bryant, 'Categorising sound and learning to read: a causal connection', made the connection between reading performance and sensitivity to the sounds in words. The early tasks that Bruce devised concerned the children's ability to hear all the individual sounds in the words, to identify them and do simple manipulation, in the case of deletion, and complex manipulation, including reconstruction, in the case of elision. Bradley and Bryant studied 4-year-old children in nursery schools, so they had to devise tasks which were not as complex as those used by Bruce. They used an odd-one-out task. This task requires the children to make a decision about which item from a group is the odd-one-out. When the task is phonological the children are required to listen to words and to say which is the odd one. Such a task involves categorisation. The children have to make a judgement about the words on the basis of the phonology but they do not actually have to manipulate the sounds. Bradley and Bryant investigated children's ability to detect the odd-one-out depending on whether the odd sound was a consonant at the beginning or end of the word, or a vowel in the middle. Examples of their stimuli are:

Beginning sound:	PAT	PEN	PIG	*WIG*
End sound:	*FAN*	CAT	HAT	MAT
Middle sound:	MOP	TOP	*TAP*	LOP

They found that children who were able to do this task went on to be good readers and spellers in primary school. They then took a group of children who could not succeed at the odd-one-out task and gave them direct training in the task. The children could be taught to do this. In addition they took a matched group of children who also could not do the odd-one-out task and trained them in a similar categorisation task which was based on semantic categories. Instead of learning about phonemes they learned to make odd-one-out judgements for stimuli such as 'apple', 'orange', 'lettuce', 'banana'. The children who received the sound categorisation training went on to be better readers and spellers than did those who received semantic categorisation training. Being able to categorise objects and spot the odd-one-out is clearly a very important cognitive skill, but one which does not relate to reading *per se*.

Inspection of the examples given for the middle- and end-sound categorisation tasks above shows that the odd-word-out is always the one that does not rhyme with the other three. This work led to the view that being aware of rhyme and being able to produce rhymes may be an important early phonological ability. At an intuitive level, being able to say that 'cat', 'fat', 'sat' all rhyme seems to require less advanced phonological skills than being able to say that 'string' without the /r/ is 'sting'. This is important for teachers because there has been a tendency in education to use the term phonological awareness as though it is a simple unitary process.

In fact there is no absolute agreement about the term or the means of measuring it. Phonological awareness is the term generally used to denote a meta-cognitive skill involving the phonological system. It is used to describe the ability to be sensitive specifically to the phonemic structure of words and the facility to manipulate those phonemes. However, authors using the same term may be referring to a variety of tasks to investigate the construct, and people using similar tasks may use different terms to label the construct (Stahl and Murray 1994; McBride-Chang 1995). Perfetti *et al.* (1987) referred to phonological *synthesis* and phonological *analysis* as separate aspects of phonological awareness. Synthesis, they felt, would be tapped by a phoneme-blending task, and it was this which enabled early reading to be developed. Phoneme blending is where the children listen to a sequence of individual sounds and have to say the word that results: e.g. /s/ /i:/ /t/ makes /s i: t/ (seat). Phonological synthesis was therefore seen as a precursor to reading. Children have to be able to do this in order to decode written words. On the other hand, analysis was tapped by a phoneme-segmentation task. Perfetti *et al.* suggested that this was facilitated *by* early reading experiences, but that it, in turn, facilitated subsequent reading development. Segmentation tasks may involve the segmentation of a word into onset and rime: e.g. hear /sæt/ (sat) and say /s/ /æt/; or into individual phonemes: e.g. hear /kaɪt/ (kite) and say /k/ /aɪ/ /t/.

Stanovich (1986, 1992) has suggested that confusion would be avoided if the term phonological *awareness* was replaced by the term phonological *sensitivity*. He wrote 'I suggest that the generic term *phonological sensitivity* be used to cover the set of processing constructs being tapped by the various tasks used in research' (see Stanovich 1992: 317). We ourselves have favoured this term (see Stainthorp and Hughes 1998). Stanovich felt that the processing constructs should be viewed along a continuum ranging from *shallow* to *deep* sensitivity. Shallow sensitivity, which was seen as prerequisite for reading, would be tapped by tasks involving larger phonological units such as rimes which also did not involve phoneme segmentation. These tasks would require the children to respond with whole words and might involve judgement and categorisation rather than manipulation. Deep sensitivity would be tapped by tasks which required an ability to segment and respond with smaller phonological units such as phonemes. This deeper level of phonological sensitivity was not considered to be pre-requisite for reading, but was itself fostered by the development of the analytic skills required for reading in an alphabetic system. Between the two extremes would be intermediate levels of sensitivity which would be tapped by tasks predicated on segmentation but not requiring responses at the level of the phoneme.

Esoteric arguments about the naming of processes may seem to have little relevance for teachers, but it is important that teachers are aware of the different types of task that may be used to develop 'phonological awareness' or 'awareness of sounds', or to 'raise phonological sensitivity', in young children.

The phonological tasks given to the children in this project fell along a continuum from shallow to deep. This was important because, as we were monitoring performance throughout their time in KS1, we needed a range of tasks for the children which would not all prove too difficult at the beginning or too easy at the end. The tasks were:

- *Rhyming* Rhyme production was assessed by giving the children five stimulus words to which they had to respond with alternative rhyming words. This is a relatively simple task where the children just have to produce other words and make no judgements or do any manipulations. Rhyme detection was assessed using an odd-one-out task similar to that used by Bryant and Bradley. However, we were interested specifically in the rhyming aspect rather than individual sounds. There were two types of set. Children had to identify the odd-one-out from sequences of four words where three rhymed and one differed either because of a different final phoneme, e.g. BED GET WET NET, or because of a different medial vowel, e.g. FELL DOLL WELL BELL.

- *Phoneme blending* Words were enunciated phoneme by phoneme and the children were asked to say what word these made when blended together. The items consisted of 2–4 phonemes including initial and final consonant clusters. For example hear /t/ /u:/, say 'to'; hear /g/ /r/ /i:/ /n/ say 'green'. This task required more than simple identification or categorisation. In order to perform the task the children had to be able to blend the sounds together to produce the word, but they did not have to do any identification or manipulation of sounds.

- *Phoneme addition* Words were spoken and the children were asked to say what word resulted from the addition of a specified phoneme. Half the trials required a consonant sound to be added to the beginning of words consisting of a vowel plus a consonant sound: e.g. *ill* + /w/ = 'will'; and half required a consonant to be added to the end of words consisting of a consonant plus a vowel sound: e.g. *so* + /p/ = 'soap'. The children were given separate practice runs for both beginning and end sounds. This task was considered to tap ability further along the continuum. To succeed the children had to show some degree of skill in manipulating sounds, although the response required was always a real word.

- *Phoneme deletion* This task was similar to phoneme addition except that the children had to say what word resulted when the specified phoneme was not sounded: e.g. 'leg' without /l/ = 'egg'; 'keep' without /p/ = 'key'.

- *Phoneme segmentation* This was designed to be the most difficult task, tapping deep phonological sensitivity. Words were spoken and the children were asked to give the component sounds in the order that they heard them. Items had 2–4 phonemes as in the phoneme-blending task. The children would hear the word 'do' and be required to say /d/ /u:/ or hear the word 'stick' and say /s/ /t/ /ɪ/ /k/. Unlike in all the

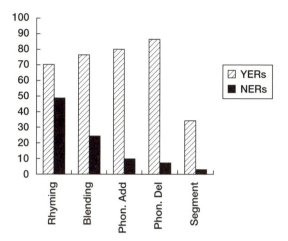

Figure 4.1 Phonological tasks: performance of YERs and NERs at 5 years of age.

other tasks, the response required here was not a word but a series of phonemes.

We had hypothesised that the YERs would be able to perform these tasks at a higher level than the NERs, and indeed this proved to be the case. Figure 4.1 compares the performance of the children on each task when their average age was just 5 years. The figures are presented as percentage-correct so that comparisons can be made between each task.

Our predictions proved correct. The children who were reading before they went to school were much better at performing these tasks than the other children. Statistical analyses confirm the intuitive interpretation. We had devised tasks which we hoped would tap a range of phonological skills appropriate throughout the time that the children were in KS1, but when we got the first set of results (age 5 years) it looked very much as though we had underestimated the abilities of the YERs, who were more than 75 per cent accurate on the addition, deletion and blending tasks. Their performance on the rhyming tasks was high, but not as high as one would have expected from the early research which identifies rhyme as an important precursor to reading. These results suggest that the YERs had a particular ability to *manipulate* the sounds in words. Their ability to add and delete sounds to and from words, and to blend the sounds together, was at a very high level. This is very important because it confirms the view that in order to develop skilled reading children need to be sufficiently aware of the individual sounds so that they can map them onto the letters. The one area of relative weakness that they showed at this age was in segmenting the words into their component phonemes.

The NERs were able to do the rhyming tasks, but they found all the other tasks exceedingly difficult. It has to be remembered that these children were matched with the YERs for level of vocabulary development and they were all above the 50th percentile. It was clear that not all the tasks made sense to the NERs. They could produce and detect rhymes, but as soon as they were asked to do a task which required any manipulation of individual phonemes they were stuck. They could understand about adding and taking away in the real world but they could not apply that knowledge when it came to the phonological domain.

Figure 4.1 shows that there was a large difference in performance between the two groups of children, but it does not illustrate the difference in the quality of the children's performance. One of the stimuli we used in the addition task was 'go'. The children were asked to put a /t/ on the end. Some of the YERs said the answer was 'got' rather than 'goat'. This mistake is very interesting. In order to make such a mistake the child had to hear the word 'go' and have a representation of it in the visual lexicon. This must have been available as a visual representation and the addition of the sound /t/ must have been translated to the addition of the appropriate letter 't'. Some children were even able to correct their mistakes on this word. This meant that they must have been able to recognise that their answer, which made sense from spelling, did not make sense from the sounds of the word they had heard. This is a very sophisticated level of performance.

Figures 4.2 and 4.3 (see opposite) show the performance on these tasks when the children were 6- and 7-years of age.

These data confirm that we had underestimated the level of skill that the YERs would achieve by the time they were at the end of KS1. They made progress on every task between ages six and seven. By the end they were clearly at ceiling, and finding the taks of rhyming, addition, deletion and blending almost trivial. The only task which they found at all taxing was the phoneme segmentation task.

The NERs made great strides in the development of their phonological skills. They tended to lag behind the YERs by about 12 months, but they made such progress that by the age of seven they too were almost at ceiling on all but the segmentation task. Being able to listen to a word and then segment it into its component sounds so that each can be specified in order may well be a task which has greater relevance to spelling than to reading, which may be why both groups found this a more difficult task. There are statistical differences between the performance of the two groups even at the age of seven, but they may well not be indicative of important educational differences. The YERs were all very accurate so there was very little variation among the group, whereas there was greater variation among the NERs.

When the children were 7.5 years of age we asked them to do a newly published test of phonological skills. This was the Phonological Assessment

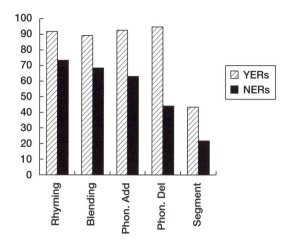

Figure 4.2 Phonological tasks: performance of YERs and NERs at 6 years of age.

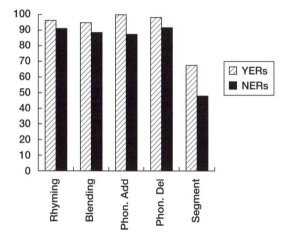

Figure 4.3 Phonological tasks: performance of YERs and NERs at 7 years of age.

Battery (Frederickson 1995). The version we used was the first research edition. The battery has now been published in standardised form. The battery was developed to aid in the identification and diagnosis of children with specific reading difficulties, so normally it would not be used with children who were performing as well as were the children in this project. However, we felt it would be interesting to validate our findings on the phonological skills of the children by finding out how well they were able to perform on this newly developed assessment. Because the testing was carried out at the end of the school year and at the end of the project we were able to assess only 11 of the NERs.

The battery includes nine sub-tests. These are:

1   *alliteration*: an odd-one-out test relating to the first phoneme in each word
2   *alliteration fluency*: generating as many words as possible in 30 seconds to a specified phoneme
3   *semantic fluency*: generating names of things in their bedrooms in 30 seconds
4   *rhyme*: an odd-one-out task relating to rhyme
5   *rhyming fluency*: generating as many words as possible that rhyme with a specified word in 30 seconds
6   *speech rate*
7   *naming speed – digits*
8   *naming speed – pictures*
9   *spoonerisms*.

The scores on each PhAB test are given in Table 4.4. The pattern of differences between the two groups of children is interesting. The NERs were just as good as the YERs for the majority of the tasks. Because the two goups were matched on vocabulary development, we would have predicted that they should be equivalent on the semantic fluency task. However, the NERs were just as good as the YERs on the alliterative and rhyming fluency tasks. Where the YERs were better was on the rhyme detection – the odd-one-out – task, the spoonerisms and the two naming-speed tasks.

A major question arises regarding the phonological skills of the YERs. Were they able to do these tasks because they were able to read, or were they

Table 4.4 YER and NER scores on the Phonological Awareness Battery (PhAB)

Sub-sets	YERs	NERs
Alliteration	9.86	9.45
Alliteration – fluency	6.14	5.30
Rhyming	18.71*	12.45
Rhyming – fluency	4.64	4.45
Semantics – fluency	10.10	9.38
Speech rate	7.59	8.58
[†]Naming speed – digits	28.27*	35.45
[†]Naming speed – pictures	46.93*	58.36
Spoonerisms	28.27*	10.73

Notes
*   Tasks on which YERs showed significantly better performance
[†]   Lower numbers indicate a faster performance

able to teach themselves to read because they were phonologically sensitive at an unusually early age? There can never be a decisive answer to this question with this group of children. However, speculation is in order. The literature on dyslexia makes it clear that there is compelling evidence for some children having a specific deficit in the phonological system, which is illustrated by weaknesses in their performance on various phonological tasks. Similarly, it could be argued that the phonological systems of the YERs in our study were functioning effectively at a much earlier age than is the norm. This may mean that they were able to capitalise on their phonological insights when they were having literacy experiences with their parents. This, in turn, would mean that they could crack the alphabetic code very early. As Stanovich says,

> early development of deep phonological sensitivity is a powerful bootstrapping mechanism to further reading progress in stages that are still very early in the child's acquisition history.
>
> (Stanovich 1992: 318)

Alphabet knowledge

Since it is argued that children need to crack the alphabetic code to be able to read they need to have fast accurate access to knowledge of the alphabet. It was therefore very important that we should collect information about these children's knowledge. But, just as there are different tasks that can be used to assess phonological skills, there are different ways that one can assess knowledge of the alphabet. In order to have complete knowledge of the alphabet children need to be able to look at each letter and identify it by both its name and its sound. They also need to be able to hear a letter's name or sound and point to the letter in question. In other words they need to be able to match letter-to-sound and sound-to-letter and cross-reference all that knowledge with the letter names. Knowledge of alphabetic order *per se* is not actually very useful in reading. However, it comes in very handy for study skills and using dictionaries. Because we were interested specifically in early-reading skills rather than study skills, we did not ask the children about their knowledge of alphabetic order. Given that we were asking them to do so much for us, we felt it was important not to give them tasks which were not strictly necessary.

We assessed the children's alphabet knowledge in all four ways plus the variant that when they heard the name or sound they had to write it. They were presented with a page on which the letters had been printed in random order. They were asked to:

1   identify the name of each letter as it was pointed out
2   identify the sound of each letter as it was pointed out

3   write the correct letter as its name was spoken
4   write the correct letter as its sound was pronounced.

The numbers set out in Table 4.5 speak for themselves. The YERs started school with almost complete knowledge of the alphabet. Indeed we would have been surprised had this not been the case. The psychological models of reading suggest that it is not possible to become a skilled reader without extensive knowledge of the alphabet. If we compare the NERs' knowledge with that of the YERs at 5 years of age we see that there is a significant difference. However, monitoring their progress over the next two years we see that by the end of the project they too had gained almost perfect knowledge. The baseline assessments used for children entering KS1 include knowledge of the alphabet, and 50 per cent is considered to be a good basis on which to build. The level of alphabet knowledge shown by the NERs as a group at the start of school would suggest that they were in a very good position to take advantage of teaching to enable them to read well by the end of KS1.

We saw in Chapter 3 how the questionnaire responses of the parents, which were used to generate the biographies of YERs at the start of the project, demonstrated these children's fascination with letters. *Sesame Street* was the most frequently mentioned TV programme, but they also mentioned the game show *Countdown*. This is an afternoon adults' programme in which contestants have to choose nine letters from unseen piles, specifying whether they want a vowel or a consonant each time. The hostess, Carol Vordeman, names each letter as she places it on view and then, after nine have been chosen, the contestants have 30 seconds to make the longest word they can

Table 4.5 Knowledge of the alphabet: performance of YERs and NERs at ages 5, 6 and 7

	Age	YERs	NERs
Saying letter names	5	25.3	10.7
	6	25.9	19.1
	7	26.0	24.9
Saying letter sounds	5	23.0	11.4
	6	24.9	18.3
	7	25.7	22.4
Writing letters to names	5	24.7	15.1
	6	25.7	21.6
	7	26.0	25.6
Writing letters to sounds	5	24.1	13.8
	6	25.1	21.2
	7	25.5	24.4

from the selection. Having learnt about the programme from the interviews, we can testify to the compelling nature of the programme, particularly if you are interested in words! Games are by their very nature trivial – but also fascinating. In order to achieve a level of skill in any activity, it is necessary to engage in a lot of repetitive practice so that automaticity is achieved. Games which are repetitive can, therefore, be very useful teaching tools.

Reading nonwords

If reading is the product of decoding and comprehension, at the start of learning to read it is decoding which is the missing factor. Children do understand language and the language they are asked to read is necessarily at a lower level than the language they speak or listen to, so comprehension of the language is not the limiting factor at the start of literacy development. The big breakthrough comes when children can decode words and therefore begin to tackle words independently.

Decoding means that sounds are ascribed to letters so that phonemes are produced which can then be blended together to produce a candidate word. As we explained in Chapter 1, the orthography of English is such that a straight letter-by letter-decoding will not always result in the correct word. It may well be that, as children get more skilled at reading, they begin to decode by using groups of letters to come up with more accurate candidates. The important thing that we have to remember is that young children are in a very different position from adults when they are reading. They are constantly coming across words they have not seen before which they need to decode because guessing will not lead to accuracy. Therefore, being able to decode successfully will enable a child to become a good reader.

The question then arises: how do we assess children's decoding skill? We could simply monitor their accuracy when they read texts, but there is no way of knowing that the children have not encountered the words before and are therefore 'reading' them from memory. Analysing the mistakes that they make is useful. Stuart and Coltheart (1988) have shown that, when the mistakes children make are in selecting substitute words which share particularly the first and last letters of the word they are trying to read, then they are well on the way to becoming successful readers. The method most commonly chosen for assessing decoding accuracy is to ask people to read nonwords. A nonword is a string of letters which does not correspond to an English word. This means that nonwords are unlikely to have been stored in a visual lexicon and so an accurate reading of them requires some decoding skill. We decided to use this method for assessing the decoding skills of the children in this project. We had predicted that the YER children would have good phonological skills and good letter knowledge. We also predicted that they would be able to use these skills to decode and thus become good readers. Their skills would be integrated.

Using nonwords to study reading accuracy, is not a matter of simply compounding sets of random letters. For example, if nonwords are to be pronounceable at all they must have a least one vowel. They may also vary on a number of different, unrelated factors:

- Nonwords can vary according to how closely they conform to English orthography. The letter string 'fron' looks quite like a real word and is pronounceable. However, the letter string 'cklepz' could never be found in English, although, as with 'fron', it is clearly possible to pronounce it. If you have just decoded it you will probably have said something like /klepz/ or possibly /kli:ps/. 'Ckle' is not permissible in English at the beginning of a word, although it is a common letter cluster at the end of a word.

- Nonwords can vary according to the number of real words to which they are similar. Because of the phonological structure of the language, coupled with its orthography, there are some words which are very similar to many other words. These words are said to have many neighbours. The neighbours of a given word are found by changing the letters one at a time: e.g. 'bat' has 19 neighbours: 'cat', 'fat', 'hat', 'mat', 'oat', 'pat', 'rat', 'sat', 'tat', 'vat', 'bet', 'bit', 'but', 'bad', 'bag', 'ban', 'bap', 'bar' and 'bay'.

- Nonwords may also be pseudo-homophones, meaning that when they are decoded the resulting phonology is that of a real word: e.g. 'teetch'.

When we were choosing the 20 nonwords to give the children in this project we decided they had to all be 'legal', i.e. look like possible real words, and pronounceable, because we were particularly interested in the children's decoding ability. Five were high-neighbour items: e.g. 'rame' has 'came', 'dame', 'fame', 'game', 'lame', 'name', 'same', 'tame', 'race', 'rage', 'rake', 'rape', 'rare', 'rate', 'rave', 'raze'; and five were low-neighbour items: e.g. 'crich' whose only possible neighbour is 'crick'. Five were pseudo-homophones: e.g.' bild' which sounds like 'billed' or 'build'. These five were matched with a set of nonwords which differed from them by just the first letter: e.g. 'rild' (Coltheart et al. 1977). We chose high- and low-neighbour items and pseudo-homophones because we wanted to see if the decoding skills of the children could be influenced by word-specific knowledge.

Figure 4.4 shows the nonword reading accuracy of all the children for the complete set of 20 items that they were asked to read at the three different ages. There is a striking difference between the two groups of children. When they were first tested, the YERs were each able to read some of the nonwords successfully, but none of the NERs could. This suggests that the YERs were able to decode words and this, in turn, meant that their good

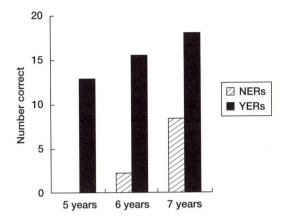

Figure 4.4 Mean scores of YERs and NERs when reading nonwords at ages 5, 6 and 7.

reading skills were generative. They were not able to read texts just because they had memorised many words. They were not performing at ceiling at this age, so they continued to make progress; nevertheless, right from starting school, they were able to use their knowledge of letter–sound correspondences to enable them to decode and successfully tackle words they had never seen before. The NERs were not able to do this at all when they were tested at 5 years of age. However, they too made substantial progress in decoding, although at 7 years they had still not reached the level of performance of the YERs at 5 years of age. Because we had used nonwords with differing characteristics we were able to examine the extent to which the children could augment their decoding skills with their generally lexical knowledge.

Figure 4.5 shows the mean number of high- and low-neighbour nonwords read correctly.

Nonwords with high neighbours look like many real words and so are likely to seem more familiar to the children than nonwords with low neighbours. Those children who were reading might therefore be able to capitalise on this, in which case they would be likely to show a neighbourhood-size effect, reading more high-neighbour nonwords than low-neighbour ones. This was true for the YERs at the age of five, but only at that age. There was a marginal effect at 6 years of age but this had completely disappeared by the age of seven. We can probably account for this by the high level of accuracy shown by these children. Their decoding skills were so good that they could not be enhanced by apparent familiarity. The NERs showed a marginal neighbourhood-size effect when they were 7 years of age. This would suggest that they were beginning to be able to decode efficiently and also to augment decoding with word-specific knowledge.

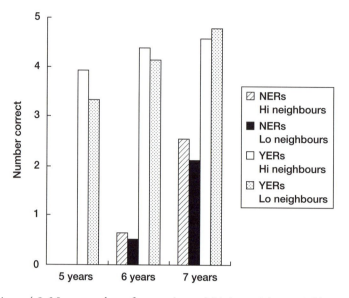

Figure 4.5 Mean number of correctly read high- and low-neighbour nonwords at ages 5, 6 and 7.

Similar effects were found with the reading of the pseudo-homophones and the matched ordinary nonwords, as can be seen in Figure 4.6.

The YERs at 5 years of age showed significantly greater accuracy when reading the pseudo-homophones than the matched nonwords. It could be argued that when they decoded the pseudo-homophones the resulting familiar phonology was useful for confirming the candidate response.

These results confirmed the prediction that the children would be able to use their phonological sensitivity and letter–sound correspondence knowledge to work out candidate phonologies for unknown words. The effect disappeared after the first year because the YERs were so good at decoding. There is, then, a suggestion that the effect is shown by the NERs two years later when they are beginning to automate their decoding skills. This is yet more confirmatory evidence for the 'Matthew effect', the spiral whereby children who are good at reading get better. The better the decoding skills, the more independent the children become and so they read more and gain greater familiarity with the letter structure of words, which in turn augments their decoding.

In the second year of the study, in addition to reading our nonwords, we asked the children to complete a research edition of the Graded Nonword Reading Test (Snowling *et al.* 1996). This test was developed because it was recognised that nonword reading could be a very useful tool when diagnos-

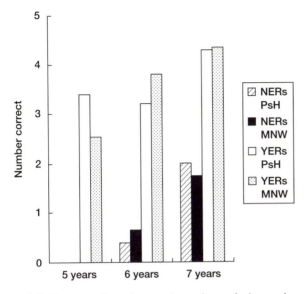

Figure 4.6 Mean number of correctly read pseudo-homophones and matched non-words at ages 5, 6 and 7.

ing the difficulties that some children have with reading. It consists of ten single-syllable nonwords and ten two-syllable ones. Our data from when the children were aged 5 years suggested that the YERs were likely to be in the very top range of ability. Since the NERs were not able to read our nonwords at that age, but had reasonable letter knowledge and rhyming skills, we thought it would be interesting to see how they performed on the Graded Nonword Reading Test (GNWRT) which has data on a standardisation population. The correlations between reading our nonwords and reading the GNWRT were extremely high: 0.98 when they were 6 years of age and 0.93 when they were aged 7 years.

The Graded Nonword Reading Test is now published and is available for teachers to use. It is easy to administer and gives a very reliable measure of the nonword reading skills of children.

Reading tests and SATs results

Attitudes to reading tests vary between people in the teaching profession; between teachers and non-teaching professionals; and across time. The view we take is that reading tests are not perfect and should never be taken as the only evidence of level of performance. However, it is often necessary to have an objective instrument which can be given to all children to enable comparisons to be made across time and groups. If one assesses reading purely by listening to a child reading a chosen book there can be no comparability across the books and no guarantee that the child has not read the book once or many times before. This was why we chose to use the Neale Analysis of Reading Ability (NARA) as one of our tests. The children read a series of graded passages, and so are assessed doing an activity which seems like a normal book-reading task; but the test allows comparisons to be made across time and in relation to a standardised population. Following the strict procedures for assessment ensures that any reading level awarded is objective. We also used the British Ability Scales' Word Reading test because it enabled us to check on the development of the children's visual vocabulary without any contextual effects. A skilled reader is one who has built up an extensive visual vocabulary so that word reading becomes automatic.

The NARA was given to all the YERs at first testing (i.e. at 5 years of age), but we did not test all the NERs. It is not appropriate to give children a test which they have no prospect of attempting successfully just for the purposes of research. Using our knowledge of the NERs reading performance, five of them were asked to do the reading tests at the age of five.

Tables 4.6a and 4.6b show the performances of the children on the NARA and the BAS reading test each time we tested all of them.

These two tables show just how good the YERs were at the start of the project: the majority had a reading age above that which would be expected of children entering Key Stage 2 (KS2). They also continued to make steady progress, which is an indication that their reading skills were deeply

Table 4.6a Mean reading age of YERs at chronological ages 5, 6 and 7

| | Reading age at chronological age | | |
	5	6	7
NARA: accuracy	8.5 (6.84–13.0)	9.66 (8.0–13.0)	11.08 (9.16–13.0)
NARA: speed	8.84 (6.42–10.92)	9.84 (7.92–12.25)	10.66 (8.5–13.0)
NARA: comprehension	7.0 (5.84–7.75)	8.0 (7.0–10.25)	9.5 (7.75–12.66)
BAS	8.66 (7.84–12.84)	10.25 (8.58–13.08)	11.42 (9.84–14.42)

Table 4.6b Mean reading age of NERs at chronological ages 5, 6 and 7

| | Reading age at chronological age | |
	6	7
NARA: accuracy	5.66 (5.0–7.0)	7.08 (5.42–9.08)
NARA: speed	6.08 (5.0–7.42)	7.33 (6.08–9.42)
NARA: comprehension	6.0 (5.25–7.25)	7.42 (5.25–9.42)
BAS	6.58 (6.08–7.84)	7.66 (6.58–9.66)

embedded and automatic and not some forced 'barking at print' which could not be sustained. Word-reading accuracy and speed were particularly well developed. Their comprehension scores on the NARA were always below their accuracy scores, but we do not think that this takes anything away from the achievement of the children. Even though below their accuracy scores, these comprehension scores were safely within the range expected of children at the end of KS1.

The performance of the NERs is also interesting. These children were clearly not fluent readers at the start of school. However, once they started receiving systematic reading instruction they made good progress. The activities of parents reported in Chapter 3 and our own evidence of rhyme and letter knowledge would have enabled us to predict that these children would become fluent readers during their time in KS1.

As we said at the start of this section, reading tests have limitations as tools for assessing performance. However, they are standardised in terms of administration to maximise the reliability of the scoring. They are also developed using a standardised population so that the performance of children can be compared to age-related norms, and progress can be monitored by giving the same test to the same children some time later (if, as with those we used, the test has norms for children across a wide range of ages). With the advent of National Curriculum assessments, children's performance is assessed relative to the Standardised Assessment Tests (SATs). The plan is that these assessments will be used as the benchmarks for national standards and, with the advent of the National Literacy Strategy, the target is for 80 per cent of the cohort at KS2 to achieve the expected standard of level 4 in English (reading, writing and spelling).

All but one of the children in this study were given the SATs at the end of the project (one child was too young). One of the NERs achieved level 2a, one level 2b, and the rest achieved level 3 for reading. Thus they were assessed as being among the very best readers in the country, achieving the top level possible for the KS1 SAT. Twelve of the YERs were also classified as achieving level 3. Two of the children were entered for the KS2 English SAT, and achieved level 4. We want to return to these two children, but for the moment we will concentrate on interpreting the results of the KS1 SAT in general.

The reading SAT is designed so that it has face validity when being done by children of 7 years of age. It relates to their interest level and, *theoretically*, covers the range of skills expected of children at the end of KS1. If we take the range of scores achieved on the Neale analysis by all the children in this study who achieved level 3 on the reading SAT, we find that level 3 spans reading accuracy ages of 6.33–13+ years and reading comprehension ages of 6.68–11.16 years. No matter how much face validity the tests have, they have not been designed to assess the children's level of reading beyond level

3. We therefore have no idea what levels of skill children in KS1 might actually be achieving.

Two children were entered for the KS2 English SAT. These two children were able to achieve level 4. This is a truly remarkable achievement. They attained the level of performance expected of children four years older than them; and they did this for *reading*, *writing* and *spelling*. One problem with the arrangements for the English SATs is that from KS2 onwards the children are given a composite score which covers reading, writing and spelling. A child who had made prodigious progress in reading, but whose writing was not as advanced, would not necessarily be able to achieve an all-round level 4. The national assessment arrangements for KS1 English therefore have no way of identifying children with specifically advanced reading skills at KS1. Concern about standards should make provision for celebrating the performance of the highest achievers.

5

WRITING

Introduction

In this chapter we consider the performance of the children on the various writing tasks we gave them. Spelling and handwriting tasks were carried out at the same time as the reading tasks. In addition, during the Autumn Terms of Y1 and Y2 they were asked to do a free-writing task. This meant that we were able to analyse their handwriting and punctuation in continuous writing as well as their self-generated spelling. Using these tasks we were also able to investigate the relationship of these secretarial skills to their compositional skills. In the final Summer Term of the study, when the children were in Y2, a further writing sample was obtained. This was either a copy of the writing sample that was used in the SAT or a sample of writing produced under similar conditions. In contrast to spelling to dictation, analysis of self-generated spelling enabled us to determine the effect of increased information processing demands on writing.

The YERs were chosen because of their advanced reading skills. When we began studying them we had no idea of the level of their writing skills. However, from the parental questionnaire responses it was clear that many of these children were already interested in writing activities as well as reading.

We predicted that the YERs would be likely to have advanced phonological skills, and so we further predicted that they would be more likely than the NERs to make use of these to help with their spelling. Although both groups of children had considerable exposure to print, we felt that the active, self-directed, engagement with texts that the YERs had already experienced might have enabled them to gain insights about the spelling and punctuation systems. Also they might have become more sensitive to differences between spoken and written language and so have found it easier to reflect these in their writing.

There was one area of writing which we could not foresee would be boosted by early reading, and that was handwriting. As we said in Chapter 1, handwriting should be considered a cognitive skill with a specific motor output. There is no reason why a child who is an advanced reader should have advanced motor co-ordination and the ability to form letters more fluently. However, knowledge of the alphabet would mean that the finished form – as opposed to the formation of the letter's line – would be more accessible.

Spelling

In order to monitor spelling development we gave the children a series of tasks. These included a standardised spelling test; a controlled free-writing task for assessing self-generated spelling vocabulary; spelling a set of words chosen in order for us to examine the spelling of vowels; and spelling nonwords.

The mean spelling ages of the children using the BAS Spelling Scale (Elliot 1992) are shown in Table 5.1.

From this we can see that the YERs were always in advance of the NERs. However, the gap in spelling ability between the two groups was not as wide as for reading. By the end of KS1 the NERs had achieved the level of spelling accuracy of the YERs at the start of the project. In other words, there was a two-year gap between the two groups. The performance of the NERs on reading and spelling was balanced, whereas the YERs showed a consistent lag between their reading and spelling ages. The range of scores for the YERs was wider than for the NERs and became considerably wider by Y2.

Error analysis of spelling mistakes

Obviously it is important that children learn to spell words correctly, but in the early stages of writing development they make lots of errors. These errors are useful for giving insights into the strategies that children use for generating possible spellings of words about which they are uncertain.

All the errors, both when doing the spelling test and during the free-writing tasks, were analysed for their similarities, both visually and phonologically, to the intended target words. Two systems for analysing the words had to be used. Intuitively, an error such as 'nyf' is phonologically

Table 5.1 Mean BAS spelling age of YERs and NERs at chronological ages 5, 6 and 7

| | *Spelling age at chronological age* | | |
	5	6	7
YERs	7.58 (6.75–9.42)	8.84 (7.16–12.08)	10.16 (7.84–14.66)
NERs		6.84 (6.00–7.42)	7.08 (7.33–9.25)

Note
Figures in parentheses represent the range of achievement from lowest to highest spelling age at each time of testing.

more or less the same as the target 'knife', but is visually quite different. However, 'kinfe' is close visually but further away phonologically.

Bruck and Waters (1988) developed a system for working out the visual accuracy of an error relative to its target. The target word is given a score depending on the number of letters and bigrams it has (a bigram being a unit of two consecutive letters). Thus the word 'light' has a score of 9, made up of five for the letters l - i - g - h - t and four for the bigrams li, ig, gh, ht. (A word will always have a score of n + (n − 1), where n is the number of letters.) The misspelling is then examined to see how many letters and bigrams it shares with the target. If 'light' is misspelled as 'liet' it shares three letters, l - i - t, and one bigram, li, with the target, and so gets a score of 4. The visual-accuracy score for a word then is the ratio of the two scores, in this case 4/9, or 0.44. If 'light' is spelled 'liht' the score will be 4 (l - i - h - t) plus 2 (li, ht) making 6. This gives a visual accuracy score of 6/9, or 0.67.

We will now use the formula to work out the visual accuracy scores for the two misspellings of knife: 'nyf' and 'kinfe':

$$\text{'nyf'} = \frac{2 + 0}{9} = \frac{2}{9} = 0.22 \qquad \text{and} \qquad \text{'kinfe'} = \frac{5 + 1}{9} = \frac{6}{9} = 0.67.$$

This gives us a way of calculating objectively what we feel intuitively, namely that 'liht' and 'kinfe', respectively, *look* more like 'light' and 'knife' than 'liet' and 'nyf'.

As a completely separate analysis we also devised a system for reflecting the degree of overlap between the phonemes represented in the misspellings and those in the target word as it would be spoken. This was the phonological accuracy score. The number of phonemes acceptably represented in the error was divided by the number of phonemes in the target. Acceptable representations of phonemes were the most usual ones described in Gimson (1962), with the application of some positional constraints. For example, the phoneme /k/ is usually represented by the letters 'ck' when it is preceded by a short vowel sound: e.g. *lick, peck, back*. When it is preceded by a long vowel sound it is represented by the letter 'k': e.g. *like, peak, bake*. There are positional constraints such that the sound /'k'/ at the beginning of a word is *never* represented by the letters 'ck'. Growing knowledge of how the orthographic system works will lead to an increase in errors which take account of positional constraints; and as spelling accuracy increases so both the visual and phonological scores will approach the full score of 1.

If we take the misspelling of 'light' as 'liht' then we find that, since 'light' has three phonemes /l/ /aɪ/ /t/, two of these, /l/ and /t/, are acceptably represented, so the phonological accuracy score is 2/3, or 0.67. However, the misspelling 'liet' represents all the phonemes acceptably and so gets a score of 3/3, or 1. Similarly 'kinfe' represents the phonemes /aɪ/ and /f/ correctly and so gets a score of 2 out of 3, or 0.67; but 'nyf' represents all three phonemes, so gets a score of 1.

We have gone into this in some detail because it is important to recognise that different strategies may be applied to different attempts at spelling words, and we need to consider all the possible strategies that might be used at different stages.

When we had analysed all the errors and given each a visual and a phonological score it was possible to investigate the changing pattern of errors made by the children. This is shown in Figure 5.1.

Misspellings such as 'liht' and 'nyf', each of which can be pronounced as the target word by applying phoneme–grapheme correspondence rules which do not violate positional constraints, are sometimes called constrained errors. Figure 5.2 shows the percentage of such errors.

It can be seen, not surprisingly, that both groups of children showed improvement over the time they were in KS1. Also, both groups showed greater phonological accuracy than visual accuracy, indicating that they were making considerable use of sound–letter correspondences. However, visual accuracy also improved along with the percentage of constrained errors, which is also an indication of growing awareness of the visual aspects of spelling. The NERs showed a two-year lag in visual accuracy, but made great strides in phonological accuracy. This meant that at the end of the study they showed only a one-year lag in phonological accuracy score. They

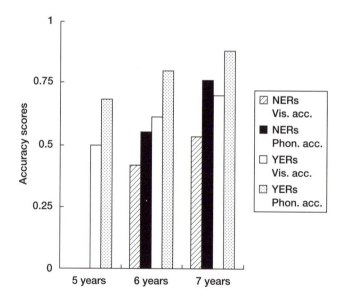

Figure 5.1 Mean visual and phonological accuracy scores on the BAS Spelling Scale: the changing pattern of errors over the project's duration.

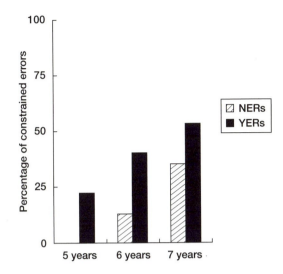

Figure 5.2 Mean percentages of YER and NER 'constrained errors' on the BAS Spelling Scale mapped over the project's duration.

were clearly developing their knowledge of the orthographic system because they showed a similarly diminished lag in constrained errors.

The corpus of words the children were asked to write when doing the BAS spelling test became more difficult each time because of the way the test is structured. However, the accuracy score and the percentage of constrained errors increased for both groups. This means that the children's errors became closer to the target words both visually and phonologically even though the words being attempted were more difficult. This seems to indicate a rapid growth both in knowledge of phoneme–grapheme correspondences and orthography and in the ability to apply this knowledge (Lennox and Siegel 1996).

When they were first tested, many of the constrained errors on the BAS spelling test made by the YERs involved a single phoneme–single grapheme match. Thus 'come' was spelled 'cum'; 'friend' was spelled 'frend' and 'addresses' was spelled 'adresis'. These were the types of error which were observed as the most common for the NERs in the final assessment.

The constrained errors made by the YERs when they were tested at ages six and seven showed an increasing knowledge of more complex phoneme–grapheme correspondences and also the application of lexical knowledge. Examples of this type of error are 'home' spelled 'houm'; 'laughing' spelled as 'lauphing' and 'larfing'; 'caution' spelled 'corsion'; and 'quotation' spelled 'quotaichon'. Apart from 'houm', each of these misspellings gets a phonological accuracy score of 1.

If visual accuracy is taken to be a measure of orthographic accuracy – i.e.

lexical knowledge concerning positional constraints and knowledge about spelling patterns – and phonological accuracy is taken to be a measure of phoneme–grapheme correspondence and the ability to apply this, then the performance of these children shows us that a phonological strategy initially takes precedence, with lexical/orthographic knowledge becoming integrated later, probably at around a spelling age of 7.6–8 years. The YERs showed some lexical influence when their mean spelling age was 7.58 years and the NERs showed this when their mean spelling age was 7.75 years.

This does not mean that words are not spelled lexically until then. In early writing children may spell some words correctly because they have learned them holistically. The spelling of these words could be said to have been achieved by rote learning, i.e. before children have acquired strategies for generating words whose spellings are unknown to them. This is different from using phoneme–grapheme correspondences or orthographic knowledge to generate a plausible spelling of a word whose composition is, as yet, unrepresented in their lexicon.

Controlled free writing

In the controlled free-writing task, which the children were asked to do only twice (at mean ages of 5.58 and 6.58 years), they were shown a set of pictures. They then had to write the story of the pictures shown in Figure 5.3 as well as they could without any help.

Nadine's first story was:

> one day a dragon layed a big egg and she was proud of it. One day the egg hached out and out poped a small dragon she was called henreata. Her mummy was called helen one day henreate went for a walk she fritend evrybody around exepet two boys who were frendly. one wanted to play ball with the dragon and they did. the dragon was good at caching the Ball. soon they were plaaying happily and they lived happily ever affer.

One year later, she wrote:

> Once upon a time there was an egg. It was a very big egg. One day the egg cracked and out popped a dragon. The dragon went to the village and frightened the people away. He met two boys with a ball. They threw the ball to the dragon. And the dragon played with the boys. he was a nice dragon.
> The end.

This example of writing by a YER may be contrasted with the two attempts

Figure 5.3 Set of pictures used in the controlled free-writing task.

at writing the story by Nan, a NER, at the same times. Nan's first attempt was:

> I saw a goterh she got out of he egg and went dome the hil and dome the tenfthe and she ferpses me werfa dome the tenfthe and she hann and got a now ferpff and it wot a goterh.

This translated as:

> I saw a dragon she got out of her egg and went down the hill and down the village and she frightened me away down the village and she hid and got a new friend and it was a dragon.

Her second attempt was:

> once ther was a egg in the hills. It had been there for a long time. But today the bady drange came out and he said. I am hurry [hungry] so he went down to the ville for some thing to eat. But wene he got there eveyonr ran away. then he said to himself. I will not eat a thing then two boys saw him they said he can play football with us then eveyone came back to see them play.

The children were all closely observed while they were writing, and any comments they made were noted. When they had finished we checked with them what they had intended to write. This was important because we would not have known what Nan had intended by her first attempt.

The percentage of correct spelling in the controlled free-writing task increased significantly when the two groups repeated the task one year later. As in the spelling tests, the NERs made sufficient progress so that at the second time of writing they achieved the same accuracy as had the YERs one year earlier. Figure 5.4 shows the percentage of correct spellings achieved by the groups at each testing, and it can be seen that the YERs had a very high level of accuracy.

There was no difference between the groups in terms of the size of the words attempted. Also it would appear that the majority of the children did not stick to words they thought they could spell. The words were therefore chosen specifically to drive the narrative. However, three of the NERs did make vocabulary changes which seemed to indicate that they were unsure of how to spell their original choice. Thus, 'clif' was written instead of 'mountain'; 'ec' (each) was changed to 'evry'; 'minite' became 'seconed'; 'playd' was changed to 'frow' (throw); and 'kicking' was written instead of 'heading' – 'because I know how to spell it'.

These editorial changes show that the children were able to make quick and appropriate substitutions. The changes are interesting as indicators of

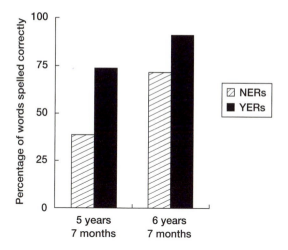

Figure 5.4 Correct spellings (as %) in the free-writing task: YERs and NERs at 5.58 and 6.58 years.

diversifying vocabulary, but interesting also because so very few changes were made to spellings either in the spelling tests or when doing the free-writing tasks when no vocabulary change was made. In the free-writing task most of the changes made were 'on-line' while the sentences were being constructed; i.e. the children immediately recognised an error and amended it. Changes made as the children read through the finished writing were less frequent.

The YERs often commented on their spellings. For example, Jeremy, having spelled 'village' as 'ville', said: 'I'll just have to squeeze the G in.' Henrietta, having written 'daisy' for 'dinosaur', remarked: 'I've got a doll called Daisy', and added 'ny' to give 'daisny'. This indicates that she could clearly recognise that she had written 'daisy', and we know from her performance on the phonological awareness tasks that she would have no problem in discriminating between 'daisy' and 'dinosaur'; yet she was quite content to allow the attempt to remain largely unchanged.

Numerous observations were made during the course of the task. For example, on spelling 'people' at the second attempt as 'peple' (his first spelling of it had been 'pellpe'), Jeremy commented: 'Perhaps I was wrong about people', but he did not go back and change his earlier attempt. The NERs were less likely to comment on their spellings. However, Mark, on writing 'ther', said: 'No, that's not *they*', and changed it to 'thay'. Other changes made by NERs included 'opnd' changed to 'opend'; 'then' changed to 'there' (this was not a vocabulary change); 'bos' to 'boys'; 'pladyed' to 'played;' and 'tundur' to 'thundur'.

The above are examples where the 'correction' is closer to the target word.

However, changes made by both groups were not always closer: 'wth' was changed to 'whit' ('with'); and 'tuw' to 'to' ('two'). Rosalind made six attempts at spelling 'watch' before she asked for help. The attempts were as follows with the visual accuracy score given in brackets: 'whach' (0.56); 'whacht' (0.67); 'whath' (0.44); 'whatch' (0.89); 'whtch' (0.69); 'whtach' (0.69).

The NERs were more likely to refer back to previous spellings. That this had happened was at times obvious, or else could be inferred from the duplication of incorrect, sometimes bizarre, spellings. This strategy is evidence that the children concerned did not have the word fully specified in their lexicon, so when they knew they had previously attempted to spell it, they were quite happy to accept their attempt as being suitable for further use. It is, of course, likely that this strategy was being used covertly at other times by children from both groups. Only one NER, Mark, commented on this: 'Just copy that ['was' written as 'wan'] from there to there.' Other children deliberately searched their text for a previous example of a word they wished to write. This meant that when the target word was copied from an original error, there were a number of consistent misspellings. Examples included 'phim' for 'people', 'goterh' for 'dragon', 'auk' for 'egg'; and 'dansr' for 'dinosaur'.

Evidence that a phonological strategy with segmentation and application of phoneme–grapheme correspondences was predominant came largely from the NERs. At the age of 5.58 years, several of this group said the target word aloud and then segmented out the initial letter, and sometimes the final or other dominant letter. For example, in order to express 'got lost the mummy looked for it', Bob wrote 'g l the m l f e'; Hope wrote 'players' as 'p u' and Fred wrote 'ball' as 'b l.' Ruth usually said the initial sound, converted it to the letter name, wrote down the correct letter and then added other letters apparently at random. For example, when she wanted to write 'time' she said: 'Time, /t/, /ti/' and wrote down 't' followed by 'arsl' to give 'tarsl'. When she had finished her piece of writing she inspected it carefully and said 'I've got a lot of esses.'

Sometimes more complete segmentation took place. Lynne segmented 'away' orally as /ə/ /w/ /eɪ/ /j ə/, and then wrote it correctly. This might indicate an awareness of complete orthography. Kate wrote 'frightened' as 'frant'. She wrote 'f' first, then left a space and wrote 't'. This was then followed by 'n' then 'r' then 'a'. She repeated the word several times segmenting out a different sound each time.

At the age of 6.58 years there were many examples of attempts to represent more than the initial and final sounds: 'spotid' ('spotted'); 'plad' ('played'); cam – ('came'). Some children continued to segment the word aloud as they were writing it down: e.g. Mark said '/k/ /ɔ/ /rə/ /nə/' while writing 'corn' for 'corner'. Although some of the spellings of the YERs could also have been produced sub-lexically in this way: e.g. 'nawty', 'thay', 'friten', they gave no overt oral signs that they were segmenting and applying phoneme–grapheme correspondences.

Several children from each group made running commentaries as they were writing, which indicated that they were concerned about their spelling. Remarks and questions relating to specific words were common, and included:

> I don't know how to spell thunder (Leonora)
> I've forgotten how to write once (Kathleen)
> Is that how you write town? (Lynne)
> That's not right (Clare)
> Dragon! I can't spell that! (Ruth)

Vowel spelling

Because the majority of irregularities in spelling involve vowels, we devised a non-standard assessment of real-word spelling to assess the spelling of these phonemes. Four types of vowel were chosen:

1 vowels which were letter names when pronounced and were represented orthographically either by a digraph – 'mean' – or by marker 'e' – 'bite';
2 short vowel sounds represented by a single letter or digraph – 'leg', 'mint', 'foot';
3 long vowels – 'seen', 'boot'; and
4 a digraph or digraph with a closing 'r' that was not a letter name – 'boot', 'tear' (verb).

Short vowel sounds were the easiest for both groups: Barry and Seymour (1988) have shown that there is least variation in the spelling of short-sound vowels. In particular, the fewest errors occurred in words where short vowels were represented by a single letter. At the age of 5, the YERs made only five errors in spelling these vowels out of 90 attempts, and the NERs made a similar proportion of errors when they were aged 7. In words where a short vowel was represented by a digraph or marker 'e', both groups made more errors even though familiar words were used – e.g. 'look', 'book', 'have', 'said'. The YERs made errors on more than a quarter of these vowels when they were 5, although less than 10 per cent a year later. The NERs made errors on more than half these vowels at the age of 6 and around 15 per cent a year later. When the words were irregular, with short vowels represented by more than one letter, the YERs were more likely than the NERs to use an incorrect digraph to represent the vowel: e.g. for 'head', 'haed' or 'heed'; for 'said', 'siad' or 'sied'; for 'have', 'haiv'. Such errors indicate application of orthographic knowledge.

Nearly half the words containing vowels which are letter names were spelled incorrectly by the NERs aged 6 and 7 years. They were also likely to use the single letter to represent its name, spelling 'light' as 'lit', 'same' as 'sam'. The YERs made errors on about a quarter of these words at ages five and six, but they made very few such errors when they were seven. They were also less likely to use a single letter to represent the vowel. Incorrect spellings, such as 'liht' and 'saem', which showed some orthographic influence, were more common for this group.

Long vowel sounds were the hardest for both groups to spell. Barry and Seymour (1988) have shown that there is considerable variation in the spelling of such vowels. The YERs made errors on half these vowels initially and on around 20 per cent at the second testing. The NERs made errors on 85 per cent of these vowels on their first testing at age six and on 45 per cent a year later. Both groups were more likely to spell long vowels with an incorrect digraph or marker 'e' than they were for short vowels, presumably because long vowels are most commonly represented by these orthographic units. Nearly half the errors of the YERs at 5 years and three-quarters at 6 years of age contained a digraph or marker 'e'; 20 per cent of the errors of the NERs at 6 years and more than a half at 7 years of age were of this type. Misspellings for both groups included 'mean' spelled as 'maen', 'mine', 'meen'; 'tear' as 'tere', 'tair', 'taer' and 'game' as 'gaem', 'gime'. Several of the spellings gave phonologically acceptable versions of the target word.

Nonword spelling

The above findings indicate that children first use a phonological strategy when spelling words which are not in their lexicon. Most of the words that beginning writers want to write will be 'new' words – that is, words that they have not spelled before – and it is therefore important that they are able to use encoding skills to spell these words. Just as with reading, we predicted that the YERs would apply their phonological skills and letter knowledge when spelling. In order to assess these encoding skills, we used the same set of nonwords that the children had been asked to read (see p. 74), with some minor changes. Obviously we could not ask the children to spell the pseudo-homophones as these are real words when pronounced; we also included five simple nonwords with the phonemic structure consonant–vowel–consonant (CVC) as we anticipated that spelling nonwords would be a particularly difficult task for the children. Figure 5.5 shows the nonword spelling accuracy of all the children for the set of 20 items that they were required to spell at the three testing ages.

All the YERs were able to spell some of the nonwords when first tested and two of the NERs were able to spell some of the CVC nonwords. Both groups made significant progress over time, and the performance of the NERs at 7 years of age matched that of the YERs at the age of five. Just as

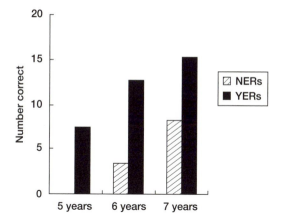

Figure 5.5 Number of nonwords spelled correctly by YERs and NERs at ages 5, 6 and 7.

with reading, the YERs at 5 years of age found high neighbour nonwords easier to spell than low neighbour ones. The fact that there was no neighbourhood size effect at ages six and seven is further evidence that the children were able to apply both lexical and nonlexical knowledge when spelling. Stuart (1990) and Dixon (1997) have speculated that because good spellers showed both phonological skills and knowledge of orthographic constraints, they could use incomplete lexical knowledge more effectively than could poorer spellers. This certainly appeared to be the case for the YERs. Although the NERs also showed no neighbourhood-size effect it is likely that this was because they were not yet able to apply orthographic knowledge to the spelling of nonwords.

As in real-word spelling, short vowel sounds were the first to be represented accurately by both groups, but all the children found it harder to represent these vowels accurately in nonwords than in real words. For short vowels the YERs achieved accuracy by age six for nonwords, but by age five for real words, and the NERs were only just beginning to achieve accuracy at age seven for nonwords. Logically, the spelling of long vowel sounds in nonwords should be easier than their spelling in real words as there are several correct representations of the vowel: thus /dəʊ d/ could be spelled correctly as 'doad', 'doed', 'dowed' or 'dode'. However, both groups found the spelling of long vowels in nonwords harder than their spelling in real words.

The spellings produced by the YERs, and their oral output as they spelled, gave some indication that they were using lexical knowledge when spelling. For example, /rɪld/ and /plu/ would be spelled as 'rild' and 'ploo' if the most common phoneme–grapheme correspondences were applied. Spellings such as 'rilled' and 'plue' indicate that the nonword has been spelled, at least in part, by the application of analogy, orthographic knowledge or morphological awareness. Similarly, although children are initially taught that /ʧ/ is spelled as 'ch' in fact '—tch' is the more usual spelling of word-final /ʧ/. Spelling /krɪʧ/ as 'critch' or 'kritch', therefore, indicates application of lexical knowledge. Such spellings became more common for the YERs over time, but were never used by the NERs.

A small number of YERs produced real word rhymes when presented with the nonwords – /fɒt/: 'cot', 'hot'; /gaɪt/: 'kite'; /reɪm/: 'tame' – and appeared to use analogy to help them spell the nonword. At times comments were more detailed: for example, one YER said after the presentation of the first few items: 'I've just realised you're adding different letters to real words: /plu/ – if you put a "b" on it, it makes my favourite colour.' Other comments from the YERs included '/slɛə/ it's got the end of bare'; '/fɪlt/ like filter'; and '/skɑn/, it's a little bit like scarf'. The NERs were more likely to indicate that they were using a sublexical route by segmenting the nonwords into individual phonemes, onset and rhyme or syllables; for example, while spelling /rəʊtæn/ saying '/r/ /əʊ/, /tæn/' and by commenting on individual phonemes, '/skɑn/ – I've forgotten what /sk/ is.'

In Chapter four we speculated that the ability to segment words into phonemes was more relevant to spelling than to reading development, and certainly the NERs gave explicit evidence of using segmentation when spelling. However, from the time of the second assessments the YERs showed increasing evidence of using their orthographic/lexical knowledge when spelling both words and nonwords. We could therefore speculate that segmentation skill is very important in early spelling, but becomes less so as a lexicon is developed and lexical knowledge applied to the spelling of new words. The latter appears at around a spelling age of 7–8 years.

It must be remembered that the NERs were functioning at least at an average level for their age and were often among the higher achievers in their class. Their performance is, therefore, typical of children in KS1, while the performance of the YERs is atypical (but gives insights into the later development of spelling).

Handwriting

The BAS copying task (Elliot *et al.* 1983) and the non-standardised handwriting copying task were carried out at the three major data-collection ages; additional observations concerning handwriting were made during other tasks involving handwriting. The BAS copying task requires children to copy a series of shapes (including some letter-like forms). For both groups, performance improved over time and there was no significant difference between the groups.

For the handwriting copying task the children were asked to copy the

Can you see the dog with the ball?

Figure 5.6 Text used in hand-writing copying test.

sentence 'Can you see the dog with the ball?', printed in 30-point Sassoon Infant font (see Figure 5.6).

The children were given a choice of writing on a line or not. At the third data-collection point they were asked to copy the sentence twice, once in their best writing and once as fast as they could; these attempts were timed. Observations and measurements were made concerning laterality, pencil hold, ability to write in a straight line, to form letters correctly and of a consistent size, and to space letters and words appropriately. (Full results are presented in Hughes 1995, 1996, 1997.)

All the children in the study had experience of using different writing tools at home and at their nursery/playgroup prior to statutory school entry. Two of the children were left-handed. Twenty-one of the children showed minor variations in their pencil hold throughout the study: their pencil hold was well established prior to school entry. At the end of the study 15 of the children were using the dynamic tripod hold and a further 3 children used this hold with the thumb slightly extended over the first finger. This hold has been described as the most usual pencil hold (Alston and Taylor 1988). However, Sassoon (1993) has cautioned against changing any unconventional hold unnecessarily, and also has remarked on the need to consider whether a traditional tripod hold is the most suitable for modern pens (Sassoon 1994). Any pencil hold needs to allow fluent writing at speed: there was no difference in the writing speeds measured at the end of the study between the children who used a dynamic tripod hold and those who used a less-conventional hold. Continued monitoring would be necessary to determine if effects of pencil hold become more apparent as the children grow. In the interviews carried out with the children at the end of the study several commented on the physical difficulty of writing: 'When you've wrote a lot your hand aches'; 'It hurts my wrist'; 'Your arms get aching'.

In the first year of the study choice of lined paper made no significant difference to the children's ability to write in a straight line. However, in the second and third years of the study use of lined paper did make a significant difference: children who wrote on lined paper showed little deviation from the horizontal, whereas children who wrote on plain paper showed an average deviation of 12mm, as shown in Figure 5.7.

Lined paper also aided legibility in free-writing tasks (see Figure 5.8), and enabled children to more accurately align letters with descenders.

Two children made unsolicited comments on their choice of paper for the free-writing task: Leonora chose lined paper 'because my writing goes downhill'; and Mark chose unlined paper 'because I'll have to write on it

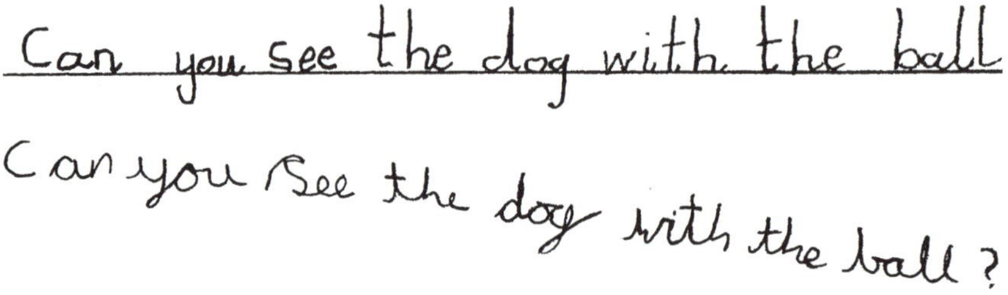

Can you see the dog with the ball

Can you See the dog with the ball ?

Figure 5.7 Deviation from the baseline, with and without using a line, at 7 years of age.

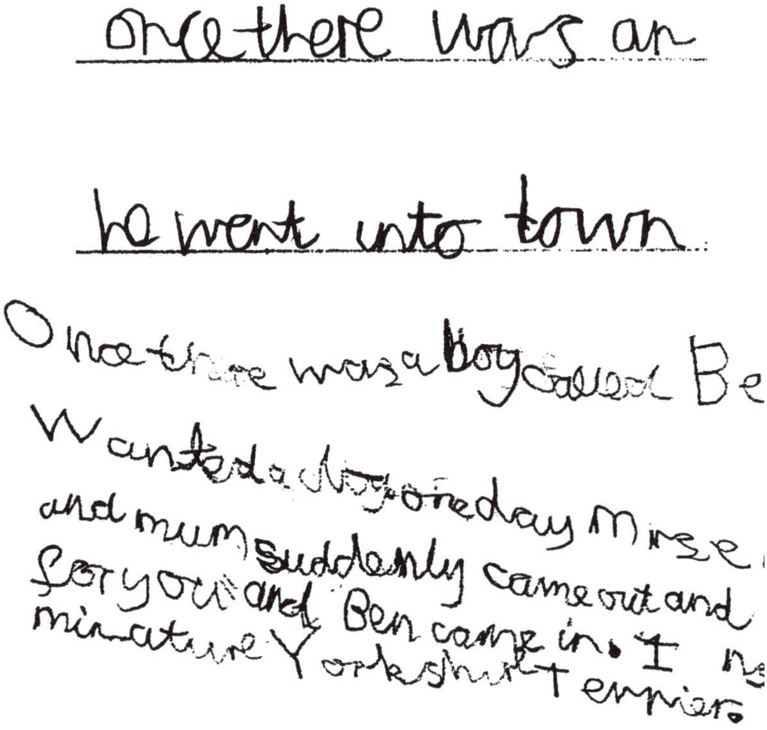

once there was an

he went into town

Once there was a boy called Be
Wanted a dog one day Mrse.
and mum suddenly came out and
for you and Ben came in. I ne
miniature Yorkshirt emmier

Figure 5.8 Free writing on lined and unlined paper.

when I'm older, so I better have some practice'. From interviews with the teachers it appeared that unlined paper was usually used in YR; in Y1 most of the children were given the opportunity to write on lines, although this was sometimes limited to handwriting practice; in Y2 both lined and unlined paper were in use. Of the writing samples collected from schools at the end of the study, 19 were written on lined paper. Interestingly the

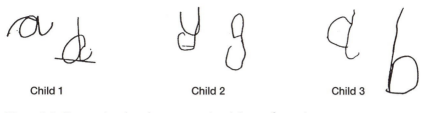

Child 1   Child 2   Child 3

Figure 5.9 Conventional and unconventional letter formation.

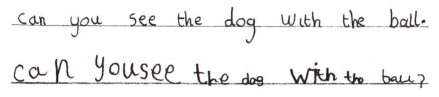

Figure 5.10 Regular and irregular spacing between words.

booklet provided for the writing assessment at the end of KS2 had lined paper (SCAA 1996).

All the schools in the study taught letter formation from YR. The majority of the children were consistently producing well-formed letters by the age of six. Figure 5.9 gives examples of conventional and unconventional letter formation. The importance of monitoring handwriting as the children practised was stressed by many teachers.

Regular spacing of words and letters appeared to be more difficult for the children than did conventional letter formation. Figure 5.10 gives examples of regular and irregular spacing between letters and words.

Only by the third data-collection point were the majority of children producing regular spacing. The use of a joined script enabled some children to make clear distinctions between words even when those spaces were small; joined script also helped them to maintain regular spacing when writing at speed.

In contrast with a study by Haines (1996), who reported that none of the final-year (Y2) infants studied used a joined style, the majority (23) of the children in this study were using a fully joined style by the end of Y2. This possibly reflects the demands of the National Curriculum: the current description for writing at level 3 includes the statement that handwriting 'is joined and legible' (DfE 1995: 20). For the majority of the children, use of a joined script was taught in Y2, although nine children attended schools where a joined script was introduced in YR. Figure 5.11 gives examples of letters with exit strokes and joined styles of writing.

If a joined style is not introduced in YR, it would seem to be important that accurate letter formation, with exit strokes where appropriate, is consolidated before a joined style is attempted. For example, Bob's handwriting

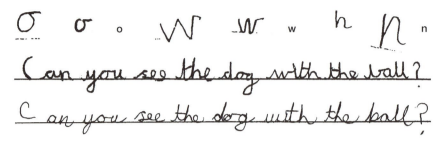

Figure 5.11 Letters with exit strokes and joined styles of writing.

Figure 5.12 Bob's handwriting at 7.3 years of age.

in free-writing tasks remained poor even at the end of the study (see Figure 5.12). Bob had been introduced to a joined style of writing at the beginning of Y2 and this caused him some confusion; he remarked at the end of the study: 'You have to do different things [in different years] and you can't get it out of your head what you did before and I cross out a lot because I forget to join.'

Production of letters of a consistent size was the most difficult aspect of handwriting for the children in the study. Overall letter size fell during the study, but a sizeable minority of children were unable to produce regularly sized letters even when using their best writing at age seven. Several children were able by this time to control letter size within individual words, but continued to have difficulty in maintaining a regular size for all the words in the copying task and in differentiating the relative heights of mid-zone letters and letters with ascenders. Figure 5.13 gives examples of failure to maintain regular letter size.

At the age of five, several of the YERs (and one NER) used upper-case

Figure 5.13 Script with inconsistently sized letters.

letters to replace lower-case letters. They appeared to be processing the sentence to be copied at a more central level and retrieving the upper-case allograph from the graphemic motor pattern store: they were not simply copying the sentence but remembering it and reproducing it from an internalised model. All of the children who used upper-case allographs had produced the upper case when writing these letters to name and sound: it seems likely that the letters were represented centrally only as the upper-case allograph. Mark made specific reference to the difficulty he had in remembering which form to use:

> You've got to do it in the right pattern [he gave the example of upper- and lower-case 't'] They're different for writing and you have to learn how to make them differently but in reading you just know they're both *t*.

Similarly, the question mark at the end of the sentence was less likely to be represented as the children became progressively capable of writing the sentence from their own internal representation. Indeed, two of the YERs replaced the question mark with a full stop.

Punctuation

There are several problems to be encountered when studying punctuation. Different types of writing will tend to generate different punctuation demands: apostrophes of contraction, exclamation marks and direct speech (entailing the use of speech marks and other associated punctuation) are more likely to be found in narrative writing and are unlikely to be used in reportage. Therefore, because a certain aspect of punctuation is not represented, it does not follow that the writer is unable to use it. Similarly, it is important to analyse incorrect usage and the incidence of omissions (i.e. where a particular punctuation mark should have been but was not used). For most punctuation – speech marks, question marks, apostrophes, commas (associated with direct speech and series) – omissions can be easily determined. It is, however, much harder to stipulate where full stops and commas (used to separate clauses) should be placed, although Cazden, Cordeiro and Giacobbe (1985) and Wilde (1996) have attempted to do so. It is also important to consider the length of the sample analysed. Anderson (1996), found that correct punctuation was sustained by only two of the 17 children in her study. These two children wrote only 4–5 simple sentences, all demarcated by full stops and capital letters. She contrasted their 'correct' performance with that of another child who used a wide variety of punctuation in her much longer piece of writing, but did not always use full stops and capital letters accurately.

The information obtained from the current study is, therefore, limited in that it analyses only narratives. The punctuation used in the two controlled free-writing tasks and in the samples of writing collected from schools at the end of the study was analysed.

In addition responses to the five items in the Concepts about Print Test (Clay 1979, 1985) that were concerned with punctuation (full stop, question mark, speech mark, comma and capital letter) were examined. These responses showed a significant difference between the groups at each time of testing. Initially most of the responses were in the form of labels for the particular punctuation mark. Definitions were not always accurate, and at the second data-collection point speech marks were described as being used 'to make it louder' (Lynne), and 'to make it shout' (Henrietta). Another child labelled speech marks as commas and said they were used 'when there's a word like fire-engine' (Philip).

At 7 years of age children from both groups defined a full stop as what is at the end of a sentence and speech marks as used to indicate that someone is talking. Two children confused speech marks with apostrophes, describing the former as 'for the end of couldn't' (Shelagh) or for use 'when you're shortening things like did not – don't' (Mark).

Only YERs gave definitions of a comma, these included:

at the end of a word that's not a sentence (Desmond)
instead of and or something (Phillip)
when you've made a long sentence and you think you've got to take a breath (Gillian)
for a pause (Florence).

Malcolm labelled a comma an apostrophe, and Henrietta called it 'a common mark, it shows there's a word missing'.

Thus, some children, even when they were unsure of the correct function of a particular mark, nevertheless demonstrated that they were beginning to be aware of the importance of punctuation in providing information.

The fact that punctuation is crucial to the reader rather than the writer makes it a difficult aspect of writing for young children, who find it hard to put themselves in the role of the reader in relation to their own writing. Punctuation appears to be intuitive for some young writers. Anderson (1996) found that Y2 children (6–7-year-olds) were able to read their stories as if they had used correct punctuation. One Y2 teacher in the current study reported that many children were able to say where full stops went when reading their own writing, but were then unable to place them accurately, without further help.

Several children were able to label, and sometimes define, particular punctuation marks before being taught about them at school. In particular, many of the YERs were able to label full stops and question marks prior to or just after school entry, and by Y2 most of the group were able to label or define the five punctuation marks included in the CAP test. As the groups had received similar teaching it has to be assumed that this knowledge was gained by the YERs through their reading. In comparison with the 20 children (5.75–6.66 years of age) studied by De Goes and Martlew (1983), none of whom were able to give the name or function of a question mark, comma or exclamation mark and only some of whom were able to label or define a full stop, both groups of children in this study showed considerable knowledge of the names and, to a lesser degree, the functions of a number of punctuation marks. This may be because, since the advent of the National Curriculum (DES 1989), greater emphasis has been placed on punctuation in KS1.

However, being able to label/define a punctuation mark was insufficient to ensure its use. Ten of the YERs were able to label/define full stops and/or question marks in the first CAP test, yet nearly three years later even those who gave a definition as well as a label were not necessarily able to use them accurately and consistently. It is interesting that although Clay (1985) allowed either a label or a definition as a correct response in the CAP test, she had previously linked only the ability to give a definition (and not a label) to fluency in reading (Clay 1975).

The full stop was the most commonly used punctuation mark. This accords with Wilde's study (1996) of the punctuation used by six children (age 8–9 years) over a two-year period, in which she found that the full stop (period) made up 87 per cent of the punctuation marks and was also more often correctly used than other punctuation.

The large number of full stops used incorrectly by the YERs at age 5.58 years, were largely (25 of 39) from one child who at times placed full stops at the end of each word, and even between each letter. Another child placed full stops (six in all) at the end of each line of writing. One of the NERs remarked, on being reminded about punctuation: 'I need lots of full stops for my writing', and placed one between each word on the line he had just completed. Cazden et al. (1985), described similar usage of the full stop (period) in their study of the punctuation used by first graders (aged 6 years).

One of the problems of teaching the use of the full stop is how to define such an abstract concept for young children. One teacher in this study described it as for use at the end of an idea or where a breath is taken. Although Cazden et al. acknowledged the latter as one of the more useful ways to teach full stops to young children, they also stated that 'the formal difficulty inherent in the scientific concept of period (full stop) should certainly make us reconsider why we actually try to teach them so early' (Cazden et al. (1985: 122).

For some children in the study use of the upper case was varied and random: their writing contained examples of both lower case and incorrect use of the upper case of the same letter. However, three of the YERs and two of the NERs at 5.58 years and three of the NERs at 6.58 years, repeatedly and consistently used the upper-case allograph of the same few letters. They also either never or rarely used the lower-case allograph of these letters. This would seem to indicate that these children were not yet making a distinction in their writing between the upper- and lower-case allographs of these particular letters, which appeared to be represented in their graphemic motor pattern store only as the upper-case allograph. Therefore, the use of the upper case could not necessarily be taken to indicate a punctuation error. Mark's comment (above) seems to reflect this. It must be remembered that by the end of Y2 all the children were functioning at least at an average level for their age, yet many still had difficulty with capitalisation

While, superficially, it would appear simple to make more or less accurate judgements concerning children's use of full stops and upper-case letters, it is in fact difficult to determine what should be deemed a correct, incorrect or omitted example of this punctuation, and also whether apparent incorrect usage of upper-case letters should always be deemed a punctuation error. This has implications for the SAT task carried out at the end of KS1, which relies, in part, on teachers making such judgements. It should be important in any evaluation to analyse both correct usage and incorrect and omitted usage, and to relate both to the overall length and complexity of the writing. It might also prove useful to consider whether only complete sentences with correct initial upper-case letter and final full stop should be examined, or whether examples of both a final full stop with a following upper-case letter or an upper-case letter used to mark the beginning of a sentence with no preceding full stop, should also be included. The latter was used in three instances by the YERs and in nine instances by the NERs at age 5.58 years.

It is extremely likely that the NERs had experienced correctly punctu-ated direct speech in their reading scheme books. Baker and Freebody (1989) reported that 'said/say and says' formed the second most frequently occurring words in basal readers, giving an indication of the frequency of direct speech which children are likely to encounter in their early reading. Such exposure may have led to the use made of direct speech by five of the NERs at 6.58 years (only one YER child used direct speech at this time) although no punctuation was used to mark direct speech. During Y2, both groups had largely the same teaching concerning the use of speech marks. However, by the end of Y2 the YERs demonstrated in their writing that they had been able to formulate hypotheses concerning the use of speech marks both from this teaching and from their reading; the NERs had clearly been less successful at doing so. The SAT samples of the YERs contained 82 instances of direct speech, 63 of which were marked correctly by speech marks, whereas only 13 of the 66 instances of direct speech of the NERs were marked correctly.

Nadine and Tamsin achieved some measure of success with the complex construction involving medial placement of the nominative clause associated with direct speech. For example, Nadine wrote:

['Look.' She cried 'A lost teddy bear.']

And Tamsin wrote:

'I think' Rusty said 'that you are very pretty.'

It is very unlikely that they had been taught such a construction, and they must therefore have formulated their own hypotheses from their reading.

It is essential to consider other aspects of punctuation when analysing the use of speech marks, because focusing on the speech marks themselves might lead to an inaccurate assessment of children's ability to use punctuation successfully. It is also necessary to consider the degree of complexity of the construction being attempted.

In the SAT samples collected, ten of the YERs and eight of the NERs used an apostrophe, to denote contraction, either correctly (Don't be so silly she said.) or incorrectly ('Ive' got to go' I said.). That is, they showed an awareness of this use of the apostrophe, although few teachers specifically stated that they had taught it.

Bryant, Devine, Ledward and Nunes (1997) maintain that children in their study found the use of the apostrophe for contraction to be easier than its use to mark possession. Only a small number of examples of use of the apostrophe were examined, but the YERs had more correct uses of the apostrophe for contraction and fewer incorrect uses and omissions than did the NERs. However, both groups made errors and omissions. The 9–11-year-old children in Bryant et al.'s study continued to find the use of the apostrophe with genitive nouns problematic and had rarely used it prior to being taught. Even the older children often left it out or put it at the end of plurals. One could speculate that one of the reasons for this is that the possessive use of the apostrophe generally occurs far less than the contraction usage in the reading material of younger children. Few of the children in this study had been taught how to use the apostrophe to mark possession, yet seven correct uses were made by two of the YERs in the SAT sample. The children appeared to be constructing hypotheses about the use of the apostrophe from their reading. Bryant et al. also found that the understanding and use of the apostrophe was related to spelling age. The mean spelling age of the YERs when the SAT sample was collected was at least 10.16 years (range 7.84–14.16 years), and that of the NERs 7.75 years (range 7.08–9.25 years).

Martens and Goodman (1996) stressed the importance of reading in the development of punctuation. They believed that teachers need to focus on how authors use punctuation, in both group and individual reading sessions. Wilde (1996) suggested that development of skill in punctuation was likely to come (for older, more proficient, users), not only through their reading of more sophisticated material but also through writing texts of increasing range and complexity. Several teachers in this study also remarked on the use of reading. Certainly in the current study some of the YERs in particular appeared to be forming hypotheses concerning punctuation from their reading.

Cazden *et al.* (1985) believed that progress in the learning of punctuation was not steady, that children's hypotheses were not fixed and that correct usage may be followed by incorrect usage and omissions. They also agreed with Scardamalia (1981) that writing is a complex activity, and stated: 'attention at one level can divert attention from another level, and make previously demonstrated knowledge temporarily disappear from performance' (Cazden *et al.* 1985: 123).

In this study, although length and complexity of writing did not necessarily equate with successful punctuation, there were several children who used correct punctuation for the first few sentences but were not able to maintain this. This applied particularly to one YER and three NERs, and accords with the work of Anderson (1996). The teacher of the YER reported that she often started off her writing using short sentences, clearly demarcated with capital letters and full stops, but that punctuation deteriorated as 'her writing starts to flow'. This perhaps reflects the dissonance noted by the teachers in Robinson's study, who felt that there was a contradiction between writing fluently and inserting correct punctuation (Robinson 1996).

We need also to consider whether, as with spelling, children find it difficult to determine where they have made errors in punctuation and, perhaps more importantly, if they find it difficult or impossible to determine where punctuation is missing.

In view of the above, it is interesting that the programmes of study for writing in the National Curriculum KS1 state: 'Pupils should be . . . consistent in their use of capital letters, full stops and question marks . . . ' (DfE 1995: 9). More research into children's writing development is needed to validate such a statement.

Composition

In Chapter 1 we gave reasons for thinking that although skilled writers focus attention on the compositional aspects of writing, for beginning writers the secretarial aspects of writing might take precedence. In this chapter we have seen that although the YERs' spelling and punctuation were in advance of those of the NERs, there was no difference in their performance in handwriting. They found the physical act of writing as hard as did their peers.

We wanted to see whether the YERs were able to allot more of their processing capacity to composition. To that end, the controlled free-writing samples were analysed to determine the complexity of the structures used by the children, and a readability score was given to each sample. It was possible to interpret what several of the NERs had written at 5.58 years only because detailed observations were made as the children had carried out the task and transcriptions made of spoken and written output. There was no difference between the groups in the length of writing sample produced, but at both times of testing the samples produced by the YERs were judged to be significantly more readable than those produced by the NERs. In order to assess readability a group of experienced teachers was presented with printed versions of the samples, but with the original spellings and punctuation.

The samples were marked on a 5-point readability scale. At age 5.58 years, 13 YERs and one NER produced texts that were largely or fully comprehensible. By 6.58 years of age 12 of the NERs fulfilled these categories and all the YERs produced fully comprehensible texts. Although spelling was probably the most important factor in assigning a readability score, particularly at 5.58 years, other factors, such as the presence of repetition and ambiguities, and lack of or incorrect punctuation (including misuse of upper-case letters), were also important. For example, Tamsin made only one spelling error and there were no repetitions or ambiguities in her writing at 5.58 years; but she did make use of a large number of upper-case letters, and three out of the six markers did not give her writing the top score.

In terms of content, children in both groups had a tendency to provide an appropriate story opening, but a specific ending featured less often. This may reflect both the types of opening/ending used in the stories they had read and the nature of the teaching concerning story structure the children had received. 'Once upon a time', 'One day', 'Once there was' and 'There was once' were the most popular openings. At 5.58 years six children from each group made no use of an introduction, though one year later all but one child used a 'formal' introduction that they were likely to have encountered in their reading. The majority of the children (eight YERs and nine NERs), however, did not provide a specific ending for their stories, simply finishing with a description of the final picture (see Figure 5.3). The conventional 'and lived happily ever after . . .' was used by only three of the YERs in the first sample and one child from each group in the second sample. The remaining children made inferences in their closing sentences, for example:

'And soon they were the best of friends!' (Tamsin).
'The D[r]agon had fun so did the boy's' (Paul).
'All the people were amazed to see the boys playing with the dragon' (Clarissa).

The pepull [people] looked out and how amost [amazed] they
weae [were] (Joe).

Nearly all of the children made non-literal references (as above) and did not
limit their story writing to a description of the pictures. Several children
wrote 'The end' when they had finished writing.

Perera (1984) found that determiner errors involving the use of 'a' rather
than 'an' before a word beginning with a vowel were found in children as
old as 11 years. This error was found significantly more often in the NERs
and may indicate that they were writing on a word-by-word basis and not
considering the words to follow. In both groups there was more frequent use
of an 'incorrect' definite article to introduce a new noun at 5.58 years than at
6.58 years. In their second writing samples the children showed increased
awareness of the convention that an indefinite article is used to introduce a
new noun, where the referent is not specified for the reader. That is, they
were becoming better able to put themselves in the reader's place.

Pronominal reference, i.e. using a pronoun to refer to a previously mentioned noun, was more common at 6.58 years, when it was used by 13 of the
YERs and eight of the NERs. The five children (four YERs and one NER) who
were inconsistent in its use all made repeated references to a particular noun
(using both 'it' and 'he' to refer to the dragon in the story); however, they
mixed both pronouns and nouns so that it was easy for the reader to know what
the writer was referring to. It would appear that as the structure of their
writing became more complex, with multiple and varying references to a
subject, inconsistent pronominal reference was more likely to occur. For
example, Benjamin referred consecutively to 'the dragon', 'it' (four times),
'he', 'friendly dragon', 'him' and 'he'. It is therefore important that such errors
are viewed not in isolation but alongside the overall complexity of the writing.

Similarly, repetition of the same pronoun or noun (where use of a
different form would be preferable), occurred more often in the second
writing samples for both groups where the children made more use of
multiple references. Once again increasing complexity of the structures
attempted led to an increase in errors.

In both groups use of simple active verbs in the past tense predominated.
Neither group made extensive use of auxiliary or catenative verb phrases.
However, the YERs made more use of catenative verb phrases than did the
NERs at the two testing times; for example, 'decided to live'; 'wantid to go'.

The YERs were able to mark the past tense at both ages, but the NERs
found this difficult at 5.58 years, even though a past tense was deemed to
have been marked correctly if the main elements of the past tense were
present; for example 'fritend' was classified as a correct past tense of
'frightened', but 'frant' was not. At this point, the NERs had their greatest
success when attempting to write common irregular past tenses, such as
'was', 'went', 'ran', 'had', 'came', 'got' and 'saw': 26 of their 32 'correct' past

tenses were in this group, and included 'ws' for 'was' and 'hd' for 'had'. This highlights the interrelationship of the various strands of writing – did the NERs represent more of these verbs 'correctly' because they are easier to spell, because they are more common or because they had been taught how to spell them?

Examination of regular past tenses also reveals this interrelationship. The YERs produced significantly more correct '—ed' endings and significantly fewer incorrectly marked endings for regular past-tense verbs than the NERs, at both 5.58 years and 6.58 years. Bryant and Nunes (1997) described the spelling of such verbs, e.g. 'crackt' for 'cracked', as part of stage 2 of their 5-stage model of spelling regular past tenses. They stated that children at this stage were not yet aware of the grammatical basis of the '—ed' ending, but spelled phonetically; '—ed' spelled as '—d' ('playd') and as '—id' ('wantid') could also be considered to belong to this (phonetic) stage, although Bryant and Nunes do not specify this. They found that phonetic spellings decrease between the ages of seven and eight as children become more aware of and sensitive to grammatical distinctions. In the current study, the majority of the spellings of regular past tenses by the YERs in the first writing sample had an '—ed' ending and only eight of 36 attempts used a phonetic spelling. Their mean spelling age at this time would have been greater than 8 years. At 6.58 years, the YERs spelled 45 of the 48 regular past tenses using '—ed' (and their mean spelling age would have been over 9 years). They appear to have acquired an awareness that regular past-tense endings are spelled '—ed' regardless of pronunciation; i.e. they were aware of the grammatical basis of the '—ed' ending. As they were only at the beginning of Y2 at the time these data were collected, it is unlikely that they would have been taught this, and it is therefore possible that they had deduced it from their reading. In contrast, the majority of the spellings by the NERs at 5.58 years fell into Bryant and Nunes' stage 1 (unsystematic spelling of word endings) or stage 2 (phonetic spelling, no conventional spellings). Nineteen of their spellings could be classified as stage 1 and eight as stage 2. At 6.58 years, 27 of their spellings would be in stages 1 and 2, but they also produced 20 correct '—ed' endings. The mean spelling age of the NERs at this time would have been 7+ years, and this accords with the finding of Bryant and Nunes that phonetic spelling of verb endings declines between 7 and 8 years of age.

The majority of the children at both testings used at least one redundant connective (usually 'and'):

> . . . and then they met tomen [two men] and he played ball and they lived . . . (Philip, 5.58 years).

> . . . and the eg hachd [hatched] and a big dragn camawt [came out] and the dragn went to a town . . . (Don, 6.58 years).

These connectives were not strictly required because the discourse was following a chronological pattern. Perera (1984) described such usage by young writers as an attempt to keep the writing moving forwards. As the children were unlikely to have encountered such usage in their reading it indicates perhaps that young writers are unable to reflect on what they have already written because all available processing capacity is being used in producing the current word.

The YERs used some complex sentences in the first free-writing task, while the NERs did not. This also seems to indicate that the latter were having to use much of their processing capacity on their spelling even though this was often primitive, with initial sounds only represented. By 6.58 years, the spelling of the NERs was more complex but seemed to be easier for them than it had been, leaving more processing capacity available for the compositional aspects of writing, thus they started to use complex sentences. It is interesting that because the YERs used so little direct speech, they used a correspondingly smaller proportion of nominative clauses. However, only the YERs produced relative clauses, albeit the easiest ones, in both the writing tasks. Such clauses are least likely to occur in the writing of younger children. Complex sentences included:

> . . . and saw it was a findle [friendly] dragen . . . (Jeremy, 5.58 years).
> While he was away the egg hached . . . (Rosalind, 6.58 years).
> . . . he said to himself. I will not eat a thing . . . (Nan, 6.58 years).
> The dragon said can I play with you . . . (Clare, 6.58 years).

It is interesting to contrast the use of the nominative clause for indirect speech made by one child from each group at 6.58 years. Gillian used the construction correctly, but Joe showed a transitional stage between direct and indirect speech: 'They asked him if he wanted to play . . .' (Gillian) and '. . . and ake [ask] did he want to play ball . . .' (Joe).

In the first controlled free-writing task, only a small number of the YERs made use of (other) structures more usually characteristic of mature writers, such as ellipsis and adverbial fronting. However, by the second writing task there was little difference between the groups in this respect, a further indication of the level of processing capacity needed initially by the NERs for the secretarial aspects of writing. Examples at age 6.58 years included: 'out popped a dragon' (Nadine); and 'One day on a clif there was an egg' (Bob).

Both groups made extensive use of prepositions and prepositional phrases, with adjectives and adverbs used far less often; there was no significant difference between the groups.

As with spelling in the controlled free-writing tasks, few stylistic changes were made: three YERs in the first task, and five YERs and seven NERs in the second task, made changes. These changes usually involved the addition of a word or the deletion of a repeated word. Most errors were not altered.

We saw in Chapter 4 that two of the YERs achieved level 4 in the KS2 English SAT. In the KS1 SAT for writing, five of the YERs achieved level 3; five achieved level 2a and two achieved level 2b. Their performance in writing did not match their performance in reading. A similar difference in performance was found in the NERs. One child achieved level 3; seven achieved level 2a; five level 2b and one level 2c.

Finally, we must comment on the length of time young children can take to write. The mean writing speed for the writing task at 6.58 years was 3.92 words per minute (there was no significant difference between the groups). This was much slower than the speed of writing in the copying task: 9.41 wpm for 'best' writing and 15.75 wpm for 'fast' writing. That writing can be a slow process for children was well summed up by Mark, who said that, although he liked writing, 'it takes me so long, by the time I've finished it's time to go home'.

6

TEACHER INTERVIEWS

Introduction

In this chapter we report on the interviews that were held with the teachers of the children. Interviews were held at the end of each year of the project. We interviewed the YR teachers only if the children had been in their class for at least two terms.

The purpose of the interviews was to find out how the teachers were catering for the needs of these children, particularly in relation to reading materials, the teaching of phonics and their strategies for hearing the children read. We also wanted to know what different provision, if any, was made for writing. When the children were in YR, they were technically too young to undergo tuition according to the National Curriculum using the programmes of study for English. However, since we knew that they were reading at least at the level expected of children at the end of KS1, we were interested to know what reference, if any, the teachers were making to these programmes of study to guide their decisions about provision. Once the children were in Y1 and Y2, they would be working under the programmes of study, so it was important also to find out whether these teachers were making use of the programmes when planning for the YERs in their classes. In addition we were interested to find out what the teachers felt were the advantages across the broad curriculum of being able to read so well so early. Finally, we wanted to know whether the YERs' reading skill had had any impact on the teachers, the class as a whole or other individuals in the class.

Reading materials

Year R teachers

Finding appropriate reading matter for young fluent readers is a perennial problem. Books written for children to read independently at the age of five, and which therefore are in tune with their emotional, cognitive and experiential levels, tend to be limited in terms of their vocabulary, syntax and length, simply because the average 5-year-old does not have a large enough recognition vocabulary or sufficient decoding skills to read lengthy texts. Such books are not sufficiently satisfying for children who are already fluent. However, young fluent readers may not have the emotional or cognitive maturity to read books written for their level of reading skill.

From the interviews it appeared that for schools using a graded reading scheme, one solution was simply to provide books at the appropriate level from the graded system. This ensured that the teacher had a measure of control of the reading matter. Because of the level of skill of the YERs a YR teacher in some instances, had to go to Y1 or Y2 teachers to request suitable books. Inevitably, the reading scheme-materials, colour-coded reading books and class library books in a YR class are chosen to reflect the expected range of skill. Sharing among teachers thus becomes a necessity where children have unexpectedly advanced skills. However, two teachers reported that their colleagues were initially sceptical about the level of ability being reported.

All the schools in the study had a policy of providing children with books to take home to read, and the majority of the YERs were encouraged to take home more than one book. Even at this early stage the teachers were reporting the children's need of more satisfyingly, 'meaty' books and so were encouraging them to take home and read 'chapter' books. A solution adopted by more than one teacher was to resource a child's needs by providing from her private collection of children's books.

Gillian's teacher was particularly insightful. The school used the Oxford Reading Tree as its central reading scheme, with a wide range of parallel colour coded-books for consolidation. Gillian's teacher used books from Y2 and checked them for both reading accuracy and comprehension levels. This teacher recognised the problem of a potential mismatch between Gillian's advanced reading ability and her general comprehension level and so was very careful in her provision. She did not simply give Gillian a free choice since she felt that guided help was particularly important at this young age. She was one of the teachers who tried providing chapter books early on because she was concerned to maintain motivation. Experienced teachers of young children are aware of the lure of 'chapters': they seem so grown up, and enable the child to read a substantial text in digestible chunks. However, Gillian herself was not particularly happy with chapter books, preferring to read a larger number of smaller books. Tamsin's teacher felt it was important to ensure Tamsin was extending her range, and had selected a number of chapter books from the school library from which Tamsin could choose. This teacher felt that she had a 'searching brain' and needed to be given a challenge.

Year 1 teachers

Y1 teachers face a particular challenge in relation to literacy. In local authority areas where there are three intakes a year, children may enter school at the beginning of the term after their fifth birthday. This means that at the beginning of the school year, a Y1 class can include children who are almost six and who have had two terms in YR and children who are just five and who have had no time in YR. Of the older children some will have made great strides in literacy during their two terms in reception and some will have found reading difficult. Of the youngest children, those who are eventually going to find reading easy may as yet have very little skill development. Such younger children may appear on the surface to be similar to the older pupils who were slow to take off, but they will be in a qualitatively different position. Add to this the possibility that the occasional child will be starting with reading skills better than the oldest children and one recognises the level of skill that the teacher has to exercise in relation to diverse abilities.

The particular issue for these teachers was finding appropriate material for the children. Two of the children were reading books from a reading programme. In both cases this was GINN 360, level 7. Phillip's teacher felt that she should maintain him at that level because the content of the level 8 books was not appropriate for his age. In addition to the GINN books she therefore brought in a supply of Puffin Books from her own collection. This was a strategy adopted by five of the teachers. Young Puffins were seen as a collection of books which provided sufficient reading challenge but appropriate content. Not all the children liked reading longer books. Gillian still preferred short books to chapter books. Her teacher had tried to encourage her to read longer books but had come to the conclusion that she was daunted by them. She was guided by Gillian's needs and supplied her with about four shorter books to take home each week.

Apart from the two children who were reading GINN books, the remaining 13 children were not reading the scheme books used in their classes. Two teachers said that they gave a completely free choice without any further qualification, whereas the remaining teachers gave guidance about the diet of books the children were reading.

Phillip was reading the Skyways books at the time of the interview. He was enjoying reading them and his teacher felt that they were at the appropriate level of skill and interest. There was co-operation between pupil and teacher because he would tell her if he was not enjoying a book or series. Henrietta had begun the year with Oxford Reading Tree levels 5–6, but her teacher was now supplying a range of paperback books that she had selected from the Y2 class. She reported a degree of scepticism on the part of her colleagues about this. They were prepared to accept her estimation of the level of word-reading skill but questioned Henrietta's ability to cope with the content. However, her teacher felt that this was not a problem and monitored Henrietta's reaction carefully in their reading sessions. The teachers reported that the children tended to read fiction books. Only Jeremy's teacher mentioned that he liked non-fiction and would take them home from choice.

Gillian's teacher was the most explicit about her strategies. She supplied a range of Y2 non-fiction books which she augmented with books of her own. She felt that guided choice was important, so, for example, she would give specific instructions to Gillian to find an anthology that included a poem about a pet. As mentioned above, Gillian at this stage preferred reading short books, but these were augmented with non-fiction books of an appropriately high reading level that related to the class topic.

Year 2 teachers

Y2 teachers have an expectation that many children in their classes will be moving towards fluent reading. Under these circumstances, the child who began school with clearly remarkable achievements may not stand out quite so much. By the end of Y2 all but one of the YERs were being given 'free choice' of their reading books (as were several of the NERs). Only one YER was still being given books from the end of the reading scheme. His teacher's reason for this was that she felt concerned about suitability of content and wanted to develop stamina. She recognised that he was a very good reader, but felt that he did not push himself. For the rest 'free choice' was a euphemism for appropriately guided choice from the range of materials provided by the teacher. Rosalind used to bring in her own books from home in consultation with the teacher. Teacher guidance was in the main to ensure that the children were tackling a range of quality books at an appropriate and satisfying level. Four of the teachers stated that they were encouraging the YER in their classes to 'choose' to read non-fiction as well as fiction. Malcolm, for the moment, had opted out of choosing all together and asked his teacher to choose for him. Recent books had included *Alice in Wonderland* and the Narnia series.

Phonics teaching

Year R teachers

When the study first started there was still considerable debate about the teaching of phonics. Now, with the National Literacy Strategy having been developed, it is expected that all children will acquire phonologic awareness and to use this to build up knowledge of phonics and letter–sound correspondences for working out unknown words.

All the YR teachers in this study reported teaching phonics to their children, and therein lies an interesting conundrum:

1   All the research evidence makes it very clear that children need to develop their sensitivity to sounds, to map letter–sound correspondences and to use these for blending and segmenting words.
2   Although the majority of children will come to school with some level of knowledge in this domain, they will generally need specific teaching.
3   This specific teaching is often best accomplished through whole-class work, not least because it is necessarily noisy – it is not possible to do sound-work silently!
4   The evidence we presented in Chapter 3 shows that the YERs all showed phonological sensitivity and advanced letter-sound knowledge, with phoneme manipulation in terms of addition, deletion, and blending all at a high level of accuracy before starting in YR.

Do such children need to be taught phonics? Or more specifically do they need to be taught the phonics which it is necessary to teach the average child? Our interviews with the YR teachers revealed that each included the YER in the class phonics lesson. The justification for this tended to be that the whole-class activity was important and they did not want the YER to be left out. Some of the teachers were conscious that this was perhaps not an ideal solution and they differentiated learning tasks when the children were consolidating their knowledge through written work. For example, Gillian was doing final-letter work whereas the rest of the class was doing alliteration work with the same letter. Her teacher also gave Gillian work to do on blending consonants, which is part of the Y1 programme. She had been introduced to activities using a dictionary.

Kathleen's teacher had recognised her ability in this area of work. She had checked Kathleen's ability to identify correctly initial and final sounds when she had started school and so, although she was included in the whole-class work, Kathleen was asked to work on blends rather than single consonant sounds. When the children were doing consolidation work, Kathleen had her own programme in which she was concentrating on spelling-sound orthography. This included working on spellings with digraphs like 'ck' and 'gh' and interesting plurals like 'ces' and 'eys'. This serves to show that her teacher felt that Kathleen was beyond needing to do the early phonics work required of the rest of the class and could be helped to use consistent letter groups to consolidate the orthographic knowledge she needed for developing her spelling. The strategy required her to use the units in exemplar words in sentences and then to combine these into longer texts.

The interview with Rosalind's teacher brought to the fore a situation relating to high achievers which was often commented upon by sensitive teachers. She ventured the observation that Rosalind did all the phonics lessons with the rest of the class and that she volunteered no more responses than did the other children, possibly because she did not want to appear to be different. The group sessions were obviously not challenging her abilities, so in the consolidation work Rosalind was using a dictionary unaided to find examples of words with specified sounds.

Phillip's teacher was aware that his phonic knowledge was very good. However, she considered that his letter formation was poor and so would include him in the whole-class activities in order to give him handwriting practice. Even so, she differentiated him from other pupils: Phillip was expected to write at greater length and, rather than simply producing letters, he was writing whole words and sometimes alliterative rhymes. His teacher felt that Phillip was beginning to extend himself.

Year 1 teachers

All the schools continued with their phonics programme into Y1, and again all the YERs were included in whole-class work. However, where ability groups were used YERs were placed in the top-level group when doing follow-up work. This was the case even when the class was a mixed Year 1 and 2 grouping. Where the majority of the class were still working on phonics for reading, the YERs were doing work which related much more to spelling: even when part of the whole class for the initial phonics input, there was always an expectation of more advanced output from the YER. For example, the YER might be expected to generate more words or to write them in sentences, while the rest of the class wrote single words.

Year 2 teachers

By Y2 all the teachers reported that their YER was well beyond the stage of needing any phonics teaching. Instead of standard phonics work YERs would be doing dictionary work and spelling activities: e.g. Clarissa's teacher had planned a programme of activities using a dictionary in order to extend her vocabulary for both speaking and writing.

Listening to children read

Year R teachers

Listening to children read has long been one of the major strategies that teachers use with beginning readers, and can prove a valuable experience for both pupils and teachers. The child gets individual attention, with the opportunity to demonstrate progress and an occasion on which to get feedback on performance. The teacher is able to monitor progress closely and have some valuable one-to-one time with the child. However, hearing children read is very costly in terms of teacher time. One only has to do the sums: 30 children in a class (we should be so lucky!) multiplied by six minutes per child equals three hours. If one listened to every child read each day and then allowed time for taking the register, going to assembly, lunch, play and PE lessons, there would be no time for anything else. As a strategy for *teaching* reading, hearing children read is a non-starter. The National Literacy Strategy requires that teachers make more efficient use of their time, so that the direct teaching of reading is done mainly in whole-class or group settings. When hearing children read, teachers can then monitor how well the children are applying their learning to texts.

The teachers in this study had clearly recognised the impracticality of trying to hear each child read every day, and reported that they would listen to each child probably two or three times a week. Most of them heard their YER read with the same frequency as the rest of the class, but two children read only once a week and one child generally only read once a fortnight.

The differences with the YERs were in the style and quality of the interactions. Kathleen's teacher had a reading conference with her with the same frequency as the other members of the class, but Kathleen was the only child who was not actually required to read aloud. Instead Kathleen would join the teacher and be asked questions about her books' content and her opinions. The teacher was pleased to report that she would choose to read non-fiction as well as fiction. In addition to these sessions in school this 'critical analysis' had been extended to homework, so Kathleen also had an exercise book for written answers to questions about her reading. Her teacher had been using this book for consolidating school work or for providing extra practice on work that Kathleen was choosing to do. However, at the time of the interview she had begun to set her own agenda and was using the book for her own purposes and writing stories in it.

When listening to the children read, word-reading accuracy was, on the whole, taken for granted, although Florence's teacher reported that she had to be encouraged to use word-attack skills. When tested by us in the spring term at the age of 4.75 years her reading age was 7.75 years on the BAS and 7.42 on the Neale Analysis so this reluctance might have been an outcome of reading aloud. Her teacher reported that Florence seemed to remember new words with ease when told them. The strategy may well have worked with Florence because she had such advanced reading skills, but it could prove problematic for a child who did not have good decoding skills and was relying purely on being told any unknown word to attempt in the text.

Clarisssa's teacher listened to her read with the same frequency as she had other members of the class, but tended to spend more time with her. The two of them would talk at length about the books and make predictions about what would happen next. The teacher was monitoring Clarissa's enjoyment level because the child's mother had reported that Clarissa was getting bored. It was considered that this might be because she was re-reading at home books she had already read at school.

Gillian was heard with the same frequency as were the other pupils in the class. Her teacher was providing her with books from Y2, so when they were discussing the books her main strategy was to monitor comprehension and to check on Gillian's understanding of vocabulary. This strategy seemed to be the dominant one for most of the teachers, who, taking accuracy for granted, were able to concentrate on the children's understanding of the themes and enjoyment of the books.

Year 1 teachers

All the teachers reported trying to listen to each child read once a week, though, if they differentiated, they would tend to hear their YER less. These sessions were very much a shared experience. As Jeremy's teacher said, she felt that he got so much pleasure from books that the two of them did a lot of talking about the content, particularly of the non-fiction books. These sessions were not used for basic skills' instruction because the teachers had plenty of evidence that when the children came across unknown words they would use their advanced decoding skills. The agenda was that these sessions provided opportunities to develop vocabulary and ensure that comprehension was keeping pace with word-reading skills. This meant that many of the teachers did not use the interaction for reading aloud unless they were particularly concentrating on fluency and expression.

Year 2 teachers

The Y2 teachers on the whole reported that they would hear their good readers less often than the children who were struggling. This did not apply only to the YER in each class, as all the teachers reported having pupils who were moving into fluency. As in Y1, these individual sessions with the children centred on vocabulary, theme and characterisation when reading the – predominantly fiction – books. Benjamin's teacher was one of several who used a group-reading strategy (long before the National Literacy Strategy), and so she had to make sure that this group was reading appro-priately challenging books.

The teachers of both Gillian and Malcolm talked about working on expression. Gillian's teacher felt that at the beginning of the year, though comprehension and accuracy were of a high order, she used to read in a monotone. By the end of the year she was projecting well and even using the teacher's mannerisms. Malcolm's teacher had a strategy of hearing the children in his class read a chosen page from a book and then using it as the focus of discussion. Malcolm therefore read more than the other children because he was reading books with a far greater density of print. He clearly enjoyed the sessions and read with good expression, including appropriate accents, whereas at the beginning of the year he had tended to mumble.

Writing

As we saw in Chapter 5, the YERs were not as advanced in writing as they were in reading, although their spelling in particular was significantly developed. Many teachers said that they expected more from their YER than from the rest of the class. This could be problematic because these children were very young and their motor skills were no more developed than those of their classmates.

Year R teachers

Florence's teacher felt that she did not like writing at length, but was able to write captions to pictures quite unaided. Her problem tended to be not leaving spaces between words, so she needed specific help with this secretarial skill. The teacher reported that Florence's mother had bought her a commercially produced book with alphabetic order so that she could record accurate spellings, but no mention was made of using a dictionary. Both Clarissa and Rosalind had been given a word book by their teachers in advance of the rest of the class. Rosalind's word book was divided into a 'have-a-go' section and an alphabetical section. Her teacher reported that she was not very keen on using it.

All the children in Gillian's class had been introduced to using a dictionary to aid their writing, but Gillian had been given her own, borrowed from the Y1 class, as the teacher felt that she was sufficiently proficient to use one. She did, however, comment that Gillian had a tendency to start writing half way across the page rather than on the left-hand side. This shows how important teacher observations are. It also serves to illustrate how uneven can be the development of literacy skills even for a YER.

The teachers were differentiating YERs from NERs by outcome on the whole so that, for example, Kathleen was expected to use punctuation and more advanced syntax even at this early age. Her teacher was also planning to introduce her to drafting. Writing is a difficult act at the best of times. However, the YERs were so much better at spelling than is usual for children of reception class age that their writing could be taken to be more advanced than their peers' purely because it was possible for the teachers to read it without interpretation. This can be clearly seen in Figure 6.1.

There is a delicate balance to be struck here. The obvious high quality of the spelling could encourage the teachers to raise their expectations of output. It is important to have high expectations, but these may have to

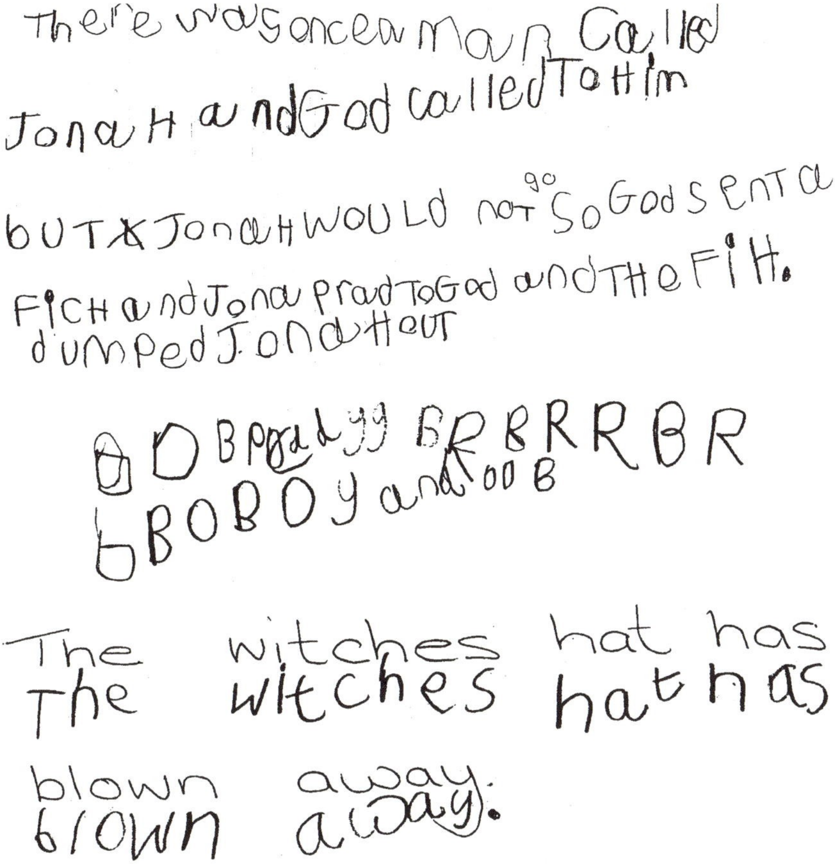

There was once a man Called
Jonah and God called To Him

buT x Jonah would not go so God sent a
Fich and Jona prad To God and THe Fih.
dumped Jonah out

OD Bpgalyy BRRRBR
bBOBO y and oo B

The witches hat has
The witches hat has

blown away.
brown away.

Figure 6.1 NER and YER scripts at 5 years of age.

be tempered with the recognition that writing can be physically difficult for such young children, and short pieces of writing might be preferable to longer passages as indicators of quality.

Year 1 teachers

Where the teachers were grouping the children, the YERs were always in the top group and, on the whole, were expected to write more and to show greater accuracy in their secretarial skills. Both Gillian and Henrietta had been moved to using lined paper because this helped them when they were writing at greater length. The teachers of both Kathleen and Phillip gave examples from the domain of science of such higher expectations. Kathleen was doing science investigations with the more able group who had been in school longer than she had (as the youngest of the YERs). Her reading

119

ability, coupled with these writing expectations, meant that she was being extended in her practical work. Phillip had, for example, been asked to collate the data from a class experiment to present to the class. In this way he was able to act as a scribe for the rest of the class. Both Phillip and Kathleen were expected to plan and draft their work as a preparatory activity.

The YERs were undoubtedly recognised as being advanced readers, but the teachers' assessment of their writing skills fitted our own. They were not as advanced in writing as in reading. Jeremy, who was an avid non-fiction reader, and whose teacher generously celebrated his achievements, was very aware that he was not nearly as good a writer as he was a reader. In the teacher's opinion, the content of his writing was generally good, but the mechanics were less developed. Tamsin found writing physically demanding and did not write at length. Her writing was technically correct, showing a sense of humour and adult usage, but her teacher felt that being left-handed contributed to the physical difficulty. Malcolm was the one child for whose writing ability the teacher had real concern: he had poor pencil control and found writing very laborious.

Shelagh was seen as a good writer. The class had a writers' workshop approach from which she benefited; she was able to produce excellent work. She was also prepared to share her writing skills with others, often acting as a scribe or a surrogate speller. This could be at the expense of her own work!

Year 2 teachers

By Y2, with reading abilities secured, the teachers appeared to become a little frustrated because the children's writing was not as advanced as their reading. Initially they tended to say that their YER was not a particularly good writer, but this was a relative judgement. Where classes were grouped, the YERs were in the top groups; but unlike with reading, they were not necessarily enthusiastic writers. The teachers' perceptions about their writing abilities tended to relate more to comparison with their reading skills than with the writing abilities of the rest of the group. There was a marked tendency for them to be better at writing descriptions than stories. Gillian's teacher was providing an individualised curriculum for her and another high-flyer in the class. They were being introduced to writing in a wide range of genres, including advertising, newspaper articles and making their own books.

National Curriculum

Year R teachers

Strictly speaking, children in YR do not have to be taught under the National Curriculum programmes of study, though in practice many YR teachers use them for their planning. The children in this study had entered school before there was a national requirement to undertake baseline assessments, although to facilitate their planning some schools were using their own entry-level assessments. Since the teachers were aware of the level of reading performance of the YERs, it should have been clear to them that they were already operating at level 2 in English – En2, Reading. Most of the teachers were not using the National Curriculum documents themselves as a source of guidance for planning for their YER.

However, there were exceptions. Rosalind's teacher had recently qualified; having just completed her PGCE. The training had required her to immerse herself in National Curriculum documents and she felt her use of them to be largely unconscious. She would therefore automatically think of Rosalind's performance in terms of levels of attainment, and would plan accordingly. Kathleen's teacher had definitely used the documents to plan ahead. She felt that Kathleen's writing was beginning to show evidence of level 3 attainment, so she was intending to try redrafting with her before the child went into Y1. Clarissa's teacher had consulted the National Curriculum documents and had had discussions with the Y1 teacher to ensure recognition of achievement and a smooth transition. She mentioned specifically checking up on use of punctuation. Given the fact that the children were much more advanced in reading than writing, we noted that those teachers who reported consulting the National Curriculum documents tended to do so for aspects of writing rather than reading.

Year 1 teachers

The Y1 teachers felt that the National Curriculum documents were not very helpful. Gillian's teacher stated very clearly that KS1 did not really apply because of her advanced reading skills, but KS2 also did not apply because she was so young. What was needed was breadth to extend and give wider experiences. Three of the teachers were using Level 3 materials. Nadine's teacher expressed the view that KS1 underestimated potential abilities. This was prophetic because at this stage the children were a year away from the KS1 SATs and her reading age on the Neale Analysis (NARA) was then 10.25 years and would be 13 years (the top of the scale) by the Spring Term of Y2.

Year 2 teachers

The picture was much the same in Y2. Though the teachers were all aware of the level of achievement of the YERs, apart from Jeremy's teacher they did not report using the KS2 documents for their planning. Henrietta's teacher had taken the unique step of developing an Individual Educational Plan (IEP) for her to ensure that stimulating materials were available, but this had not involved the programmes of study for KS2. Gillian was in an

Infant school so her teacher had tried to liaise with the KS2 school in order to develop more advanced work. She had consulted the KS2 programmes of study, but the KS2 colleagues were reluctant for her to do any work that they were intending to cover.

Cross-curricular advantages

Year R teachers

Clearly the ability to read leads to positive consequences across all curriculum areas, but we were interested in the teachers' views about how the children had benefited generally from being such good readers.

Overwhelmingly they reported that a major benefit of being an independent reader was that it enabled the children to get on with their maths work. Any maths that requires even a modicum of reading before being undertaken generally needs interpretation by the teacher at this early stage. The YERs could read the instructions, the maths books themselves and any worksheets, and so could get on with their maths independently. The teachers were not saying that the children did not need teaching: they were simply pointing out that the children's ability to read enabled them to get on with work immediately and with the confidence that they knew what they were doing. Gillian's teacher capitalised on this by giving her extra number work with written instructions. Kathleen's teacher also made specific comments about maths. She felt that Kathleen was able to ask for help in a way that the other children could not. Kathleen was able to monitor what she had to do by being able to read the text so that any help she requested related solely to the mathematical agenda.

In addition to maths, teachers reported that the YERs reading ability meant that their topic work was often of a different order than that of the rest of the class. Kathleen's teacher was very insightful about this. She felt that because Kathleen was able to read the non-fiction books on the topic independently, she gained a greater understanding than she would have done by simply hearing it read to her. By reading and re-reading the text Kathleen was able to reflect upon the content far more than were the other children. Gillian's teacher also mentioned the independent reading of non-fiction books as a major bonus for topic work. She carefully selected books to help Gillian.

Clearly, by the nature of our questions we were making the assumption that being able to read fluently was a positive attribute; however, negative aspects were mentioned. One child's teacher felt that because reading was so easy for her, she was a little reluctant to do things that she found difficult. Having diagnosed this as an issue, the teacher was seeking to remedy this by setting tasks which required her to find things out using the non-fiction books available in the class.

One teacher said that advanced reading ability did not have any substantial knock-on effects because she did not use any materials for the class in other areas of the curriculum that required the children to read. As an approach, this gives cause for concern. If reading is to be viewed as a study skill that serves the rest of the curriculum, then right from the start we need to think about providing appropriate reading materials across the curriculum.

Year 1 teachers

Again, in this year, there was one teacher who felt that being able to read had not had any implications for the YER in her class as far as the wider curriculum was concerned. However, the other teachers' comments were perfect exemplifications of the 'Matthew effect'. Although, when talking about the reading materials they provided for the children, non-fiction did not loom large, in considering the beneficial effects of being able to read so early it was clear to the teachers that these children had been reading and absorbing information independently for some time. Six teachers commented on the children's wide general knowledge and ability to read around the topic independently. Tamsin's teacher said that often when she asked her how she knew a particular piece of information, the reply was that she had 'read it'. By this stage reading was an activity that the children took for granted.

In Y1 there was again a perceived major effect on maths. The children were reported as able to read the maths sheets and carry out maths investigations in a much more independent way. This characteristic of independence was frequently mentioned. A number of teachers commented on the children having the necessary reading skills to acquire information independently, but it was really only Gillian's teacher who seemed to plan study skills into her differentiated curriculum.

Year 2 teachers

The positive effects for individuals were commented on also by most of the Y2 teachers. The general knowledge of YERs was felt to be very good and their level of reading skill meant that they could tackle more demanding work. Malcolm's teacher said that he had an amazing general knowledge – it was 'quite staggering' – and he also had a good memory. However, she was a little concerned about his problem-solving skills. Leonora's teacher felt that she was successfully using her skills for researching information necessary to extend the topic work. Nadine's teacher made the comment that she was able to read much faster than the other children and that this was a real bonus when researching topics.

There were again a few negative comments. One child who was considered capable of independent work was also a real 'handful' in class, and it was felt that he would have to be placed with a very strong teacher in the junior school. A comment that had been made about one child in YR was now made about a different child: her teacher felt that she had found reading very easy and therefore was able to access information effortlessly; however, rather than being seen as a positive factor, this effortless performance gave rise to the impression that she was coasting.

One child was described by his teacher as a 'receptive' rather than an active learner. This is an interesting observation given that he had largely taught himself to read, which one would generally consider to be a fairly active process. She said that he did not read as much as the other children, as evidenced by him changing his books less frequently. His reading age on the NARA at that time was 10.33 years, so one might begin to think about the diet that was being provided for him in school. She was the only Y2 teacher who did not think that having such a child in her class made a difference to herself or the other pupils.

Effects on the class and the teacher

Year R teachers

On the whole the teachers felt very stimulated by having these children in their classes. They did not report feeling threatened by this display of prodigious skill, but they did express their concerns about their ability to provide enough challenging material for the children. All primary teachers have to deal with a wide range of abilities and skills, but YR teachers do not always have the challenge of receiving fluent readers at the start of the term. Some teachers had never had a child with such advanced reading ability in their YR classes before. One teacher summed it up by saying that this challenge made more work for the teacher in two ways. First, she felt it most important to provide special work to ensure that the child did not just mark time; and, second, she felt that this programme had to link in directly to the work that the other children were doing so that her YER did not feel isolated. More than one teacher admitted to feeling concerned about providing the level of challenge that the situation warranted. A number of teachers were very positive about benefits that the YER brought to the whole class. As one teacher put it, she was asking more searching questions of all the children because she was aware of the level of knowledge that the YER had gained through reading. The YERs were often used as peer tutors within their respective classes, reading instructions to others both from hard copy and on the computer; acting as a scribe for others and also reading to them.

Year 1 teachers

Where the schools operated a mixed Y1–Y2 class system, the teachers felt that their task was probably easier because they were used to planning for a wide range of abilities and also because the YERs were able to work with the most advanced of their Y2 children. Henrietta's teacher said she had found it particularly interesting having her in the class. Clarissa's teacher felt that the child's presence meant that she had made greater demands on the other members of the class, and that they were rising to the challenge. Malcolm's teacher had enjoyed having him in her class but said that she felt frustrated because she had not always been able to provide him with a sufficiently challenging diet. The teachers were used to building differentiation into their planning, but the presence of the YERs added another dimension to this. In the main they had found it a very rewarding experience professionally, but also acknowledged that they had had to work harder than usual.

The perceived benefits to the class as a whole were illustrated by Malcolm's teacher, who said she felt that the standard of the whole class had been raised. The YERs were often used as role models for the other children: YERs would read to them and with them, and help them gain access to the computer. Kathleen's teacher reported that the child would read to other children, and when sharing reading with them would use the same strategies that she herself used to help children achieve accuracy. This little girl was reported as having an advanced capacity to empathise.

Year 2 teachers

Apart from one teacher who did not think the YER had had any effect either on her as teacher or on the rest of the class, the other Y2 teachers were much more positive and their comments were very similar to the YR and Y1 teachers. Clarissa's teacher felt that she was a very good role model who had generally raised the level of the whole class. Florence was seen as having been a positive influence who was pleased to share her knowledge with others. Besides being a good role model, Jeremy was seen as having enriched the vocabulary of the class because he was such a good speaker. Malcolm's teacher said that, on a professional level, having him in the class had been beneficial to her because she was now much more aware of the needs of able children. One of her concerns was that she did not want to bore or demotivate a child with such advanced general knowledge. Gillian's teacher summed up the YER experience by saying that it had been a hard year, but a very rewarding one.

Implications for teachers

We have tried to be as objective as possible in giving this account of what the teachers said to us. What lessons are to be drawn from the teachers' experiences?

There are definite issues about resourcing the classroom. Margaret Clark reported the concern experienced by parents in making provision for their children. Publishing has moved on considerably in the last 20 years, so in the UK there is a wealth of quality books written for young children and an increasing number of reading schemes with books which are equal in quality to non-scheme books. However, such abundance does not necessarily help children as young as five: indeed, the more books there are, the more difficult it may be to choose well. It seems to us that best practice was found where teachers gave children guided choice and were sufficiently aware of their needs to go beyond their own classrooms to provide an enriched but appropriate diet. One might be despondent about a system in which it was necessary for teachers to resource their own classrooms. However, this can be seen positively. All primary teachers have a collection of children's literature, and it must have made the children feel very special to be given the opportunity to share books belonging to their teachers. Another positive aspect was that the teachers were recognising the need to supply appropriate materials.

At the end of the project, the 'weakest' YER was a child who then, at 6.5 years of age, had a reading age of 9.16 years, and the 'best' was a child who had a reading age of 13+ at 6.66 years. There is always going to be a challenge to provide books that are satisfying in terms both of sheer volume of print and of themes which are appropriate for such young children to read. Malcolm's teacher had solved the problem by turning to the children's classics. It is probably true to say that these books, which were maybe written for junior-age children to read independently, make ideal reading for very good young readers of today. The books that the teachers were supplying for independent reading were often the books that they may choose to read to the class as a whole. However, there is always the issue that Gillian raised. She was undoubtedly a good reader and worked hard in school, but certainly in YR and Y1 she had not developed the stamina to read really long books. She was lucky to have teachers who recognised this and kept her supplied with sufficient shorter books to maintain her reading rate and enthusiasm.

7

INTERVIEWS WITH PARENTS

This chapter focuses on the information obtained from the parents in interviews held at the end of the three school years over which this study was conducted. At the end of YR only the parents of the 14 children who had had 2–3 terms in school were interviewed. At least one parent of each child was interviewed when the children reached the end of Y1 and 27 parents were interviewed as the children reached the end of KS1 (Y2). It was usually the mother who attended these interviews; occasionally the father also was present. We have included also such information from teachers as seems relevant to this aspect of the study.

The data collected centred around five main areas, and comprised information:

1   that parents gave to the school relating to their child's reading ability; this included their perception of the school's reaction to the information;
2   about any discussions, either formal or informal, that the parents had with their child's class teacher or with the headteacher, and the parents' views about such discussions;
3   about how parents regarded their child's experience of school during the year, including his or her motivation, socialisation, academic progress and any concerns they may have had;
4   about parents' perceptions of the school's ablility to develop their child's advanced reading and writing skills.
5   concerning reading and writing development that parents received from the schools in the form of written reports.

It is important to note that what follows reflects the views of the parents and how they perceived their interactions with the school. We are unable to include any material which might compromise the anonymity of the individual parents.

Reading ability

Parents of 11 YERs informed the school that their child could read fluently either before or just as the child started in the nursery class, YR, or Y1. (The different local education authorities covered meant that some children entered school after their fifth birthday; therefore, not all the children had time in YR.) Information was given either to the headteacher, class teacher or in written form as part of the information requested by the school prior to school entry. Four children started school after we had collected the first lot of data, so their parents also told the school about the research and gave copies of our early results. In interviews with the teachers, eight of the YR/Y1 teachers reported that they had been told by the child's nursery teacher or playgroup leader that he or she was able to read.

Four parents did not tell the school directly – three of these were parents of children who attended a nursery class attached to the school. They were aware that the nursery teacher had informed the child's prospective class teacher. One parent reported that she may have mentioned it briefly; she hoped that the school would 'pick up on it'.

The reaction of the schools varied. Two parents felt that there had been no feedback from the school. Several parents felt that their information had been received with some scepticism. Two parents had told their child's nursery teacher, and each reported a sceptical response.

One said:

> At first I think they didn't believe me. The headteacher said: 'We haven't had anyone coming into nursery reading.'

The other commented:

> The [nursery] teacher took it in her stride but I felt she was thinking 'I'll let this woman speak and find out later'.

Comments from parents who had informed their child's YR or Y1 teacher included:

> School didn't really believe it when I first mentioned it – but when I showed them the results they realised she was a reader.

> I think the headteacher was somewhat sceptical.

> The headteacher brushed it aside and seemed more concerned with the ones that couldn't read than the ones that could.

One parent reported that her child's reading ability had been noticed by the nursery teacher who started the child on the school reading scheme. The headteacher was very interested and listened to the child reading. She was said by the parent to be 'delighted to have another bright child'. Two headteachers had reassured parents about the provision of differentiated work or special programmes of provision. However, only one school had set up an IEP, at the beginning of Y2, for the YER.

Parents' discussions with teachers

All the teachers interviewed reported that their schools operated an open-door policy. Individual teachers were available to talk to parents before and after school without specific appointments being made, although one teacher remarked that talking to parents before school was not really practicable! Parents could also make appointments to see either the class teacher or the headteacher at any time.

In addition to these informal meetings all the schools held formal open evenings, most of them in the Autumn Term. These often took the form of a group meeting where each class teacher talked to parents about reading methods, maths and other areas of the curriculum. Individual parent–teacher meetings were also held by some schools in the Autumn Term. These meetings were described by one teacher as being for two-way information; this was in contrast to later meetings in which she felt she was informing the parents, for example concerning the child's Record of Achievement. One teacher said that she found meetings with parents particularly valuable 'because parents know their children better than we do even though we see them every day'.

Twelve schools held meetings with individual parents in the Summer Term to discuss their child's Record of Achievement or school report, and three other schools made this meeting optional. These three schools (and three others) had open evenings in the Spring Term. One school produced a formative (rather than summative) report in the Spring Term and this was discussed after the children had shown parents their work. Parents were reported to like this, and one had commented: 'The children are so proud. I like it this way.' Parents who had children in Y2 at this school were given their children's SAT levels and an explanatory letter in the Summer Term, and could request an individual meeting if they wanted to discuss these. One school held meetings with individual parents of Y2 children in the Spring Term so that any problems could be tackled prior to assessments.

All the parents welcomed these opportunities to discuss their child; they expressed an interest in finding out what their child was doing at school, what progress he/she was making and how they could support the work of the school at home. They attended all the formal open evenings (only two parents had each missed a single open evening during their child's time in

KS1); and parents of 13 of the YERs and nine of the NERs had initiated informal discussions with their child's class teacher.

Nevertheless, although parents were on the whole happy to approach their child's teacher, the parents of 11 YERs and six NERs would have liked more discussion, and in particular would have welcomed more school-initiated discussions. Parents were aware of the constraints on teachers' time and did not wish to appear 'pushy'. Typical comments were:

> I would have liked more discussions [initiated by the school] so that I didn't feel a nuisance.

> I would have liked to have been better informed, but I didn't want to alienate the teacher.

> I feel pressurised not to be a pushy as a parent.

> I can always talk after school, but I don't want to be seen as a pushy mother.

> If you request meetings, they are somehow on the defensive.

By the end of their child's time in Y2 several of these parents seemed more relaxed (or more inured!) about going into school:

> It's a lot easier now, the teacher's easy to talk to.

> I feel I can ask about anything.

> They're so good up there [at the school].

However, three parents felt somewhat differently:

> I'm perceived as a pushy parent. I've given up on it.

> I've decided to keep a low profile this year.

> I try and keep well out of the way.

Three parents felt that meetings held at the end of the year did not allow time for problems to be tackled before the child moved to the next class, and one parent felt that even a Spring Term open evening left it too late.

In addition to wanting more opportunities to discuss information specific to their child, several parents would have welcomed more general information concerning the work that the class was doing and how this could be followed up at home; further explanation concerning reading methods (particularly as their child's reading developed); how spelling was approached at school; and further chances to see their child's work. One parent felt that information was less accessible to parents who work.

The parents of nine YERs and five NERs had helped in school on a regular or irregular basis at some time during the study. The parents who did not help were either working or had younger children at home. The two main reasons given for helping were wanting to get to know the other children and finding out what was happening in class. Some parents felt that helping in school enabled more informal discussion to take place and that they would be more accessible to the teacher if a particular problem arose. Two parents who were unable to help felt that it would have enabled them to learn more about how things were done at school had they been able to do so.

It has to be said that the teachers seemed unaware that parents would have liked further information. When asked their views on meetings held with parents they said, almost unanimously, that they felt these were satisfactory from both the teachers' and the parents' point of view, even when the parents had a different opinion. For example, one teacher felt that a question about reading had been 'sorted out' whereas the parent remained concerned. Another parent said 'I could go along and ask [for a meeting], but I don't like to be the pain in the backside parent.' However, the teacher felt that this parent had not been hesitant about going into school. These comments concerned schools and teachers who genuinely felt that parents were comfortable about approaching them.

Most of the schools held regular curriculum evenings, sometimes aimed at all parents, sometimes aimed at 'new' parents. School booklets/brochures usually contained information concerning literacy, and several schools produced additional leaflets on specific aspects of literacy: for example, on listening to reading, helping with spelling and supporting handwriting. Several schools had ongoing communication, largely concerning reading, which took the form of a card, record book or reading diary, and usually had spaces for parent and teacher comments and often space for a comment from the child. One school had abandoned home–school cards because they were not fully used by the parents and were very time consuming for the teachers. One school had recently started a home–school book link; the teacher, however, had remarked that 'the parents rarely put anything in them'.

One school had a series of 'markers' which carried different suggestions for activities. A marker appropriate to the child and the book chosen would then be sent home. Suggestions included: 'Talk about the pictures'; 'Read the book to your child'; 'Read this book together'. One teacher mentioned specifically that the record charts kept for self-chosen library books enabled her to check that a child was choosing a suitable variety of books.

Only two parents commented on this ongoing communication. One parent felt that there was little feedback to the comments she regularly made, and the other felt there was insufficient guidance. She gave the example of a teacher saying 'Please learn these words', but did not know how to help her child do this.

Parental concerns about socialisation, motivation and progress

Year R

The parents of the six NERs who had spent 2–3 terms in a YR class reported that their child had settled in well and was happy at school: he/she 'loves it and is upset when it's the holidays', 'is very compatible with the teacher and has responded well to little rituals and classroom organisation'. On the whole the children were motivated, but one parent felt that the child was not motivated by the reading scheme and that this was not helped by bringing home only one book a week. This parent was concerned that the child was not being pushed sufficiently in English and maths. She commented: 'I've looked upon it as more of a social experience and feel she is wanting to do more than there is at school.' Two parents expressed concern over reading: one was disappointed that the child had not made more progress and one was worried that the same book had been brought home repeatedly. Another parent was a little concerned that, because her child was quiet, the teacher might not appreciate the extent of his knowledge. In terms of progress made, one parent said that her child had 'maybe' learned to be more accurate in reading, to read with expression and to form letters correctly; one parent was not sure what progress had been made; two parents commented on their child's reading vocabulary and one said that the child was confident when reading the books brought home from school. Another parent said: 'I can't see progress in writing because we only get to see odd bits.'

Only two of the eight YERs had experienced any difficulty in settling at school. One of these children had been confident in nursery, so this was something of a surprise. The other parent said that in view of this early difficulty the school year had 'gone a million times better than I could have hoped for'. The other six YERs had settled in well and by the time the interviews were conducted all the children were happy socially; two parents said that their child's confidence had grown and a further two parents that the year had gone better than they had anticipated. Four parents commented specifically about motivation: one child was said to enjoy the more challenging work that she did; one parent felt that her child's interest was being maintained but that the child was not self-motivated, preferring to chat! Three parents had no major concerns, but the remaining five parents were concerned that their child was not being stretched or had made little progress. None of the parents felt that school had been instrumental in any changes in their child's reading. Four parents said that their child was reading more widely but that this was largely from books provided at home, and they felt that any progress made was a continuation of the natural development of reading that had already taken place. Five parents felt that progress had been made in writing – either in letter formation or in quantity of writing. The parents of the YERs were more likely than were parents of NERs to comment on social aspects of school. Typical remarks included: 'School has done her a lot of good. Because she can read she has been able to concentrate on other things'; 'It's been good for her socially'; 'he is much more confident'. However, one parent, who was pleased with the child's social development, added: 'Academically I don't think she has learned anything, only odd snippets of general knowledge.'

Year 1

Nearly all the children were described as being happily settled at school, including those who had started school in Y1. Comments made by the parents of YERs included: 'he is exceptionally happy'; 'she is happy and enthusiastic'; 'school is emotionally a great success'; and those made by the parents of NERs included: 'she has enjoyed school and everything that goes with it'; 'he is full of it'; and 'school has gone well in all respects'. One child from each group had taken some time settling in their Y1 class, although both had experience of being in a YR class. Most of the children were motivated to work, although the parents of the YERs were the more likely to comment on this: 'I think his teacher keeps him challenged and interested with extension work'; and 'there's just enough to keep her motivated'. However, one parent remarked that her child was self-motivated rather than stimulated by the work at school; she said 'he is well motivated despite not getting appropriate work'. Parents of two YERs and of one NER were concerned about their child's motivation. One parent said: 'I'm concerned that she hasn't got the desire or chance to progress.' This parent and one other would have liked the schools to define their child's needs and provide a structured plan, 'not extra bits here and there'. The parent of another NER felt that the classroom itself was not a motivating environment.

The parents of five YERs and nine NERs had no real concerns about their child's schooling during Y1. The parents of four NERs were concerned about literacy, mentioning reading, spelling and handwriting. Parents of five YERs questioned whether their child was being stretched enough, one adding that she was concerned that, because her child had never had to do difficult things, she had not developed a strategy for tackling them. The parent of a YER mentioned spelling, and another was concerned that the books her child was required to read were not challenging.

The parents of seven YERs and nine NERs referred to progress made in reading. For the YERs this was described largely as a change in the type of material read: 'he is reading more broadly'; 'she is reading denser texts'; 'she has made a good attempt at reading cursive [hand-written] script'; although one parent remarked that her child's reading was extending his vocabulary and that he would ask the meaning of new words he encountered. The parents of NERs were the more likely to make a general comment about reading: 'reading has come on in leaps and bounds'; 'reading has suddenly clicked'; 'reading is going well'; or to comment on strategies used: 'he can now read his reading-scheme book and is no longer looking at the pictures and making up the story'; 'she chooses to read now, but uses picture clues rather than other strategies'.

The parents of ten YERs and five NERs mentioned progress in writing. The comments of the parents of the YERs included: 'the mechanics of handwriting are sorted out now'; 'writing has leapt ahead'; 'writing can be neat and she writes imaginative stories'; 'he is writing more and also more maturely'. The parents of NERs said: 'he will attempt words he doesn't know how to spell'; 'writing has improved but has a lot further to go than with reading'; 'she likes to be an independent writer'.

Parents of two YERs found it difficult to judge what progress had been made and one felt there was no change in her child's reading and writing. Parents of two NERs were disappointed in the progress made by their child.

Parents of two children from each group referred to more general changes: 'she asks more questions and remembers things a lot better'; 'her interests are a lot more grown up'.

Year 2

All the children settled well in their Y2 classes and most of the parents made positive comments about their child's time in Y2, their motivation and socialisation: 'A good year, she is a pleasure to be around'; 'Marvellous. I couldn't be more pleased'; 'Wonderful, he loves it'; 'he is happy and his concentration has improved'. Parents of two YERs were less enthusiastic: one felt that the year had been unsatisfactory, the other that, although her child had been enthused by the topics covered, the work was too easy. The parent of one NER said that, although the year had gone 'quite well', her child was bored at the moment; however, she speculated that this might be because the pupils had just carried out their Standardised Assessment Tests!

On the whole parents had few concerns. One parent from each group was concerned that the child was in a mixed Y1–Y2 class. The parent of a YER was concerned generally about the child's education and progress even though the child was happy at school. Three YERs were described as a little apprehensive about the move to junior school, and one YER was said to 'switch off' at school at times: her mother said, laughing: 'She gets a bit of a rest at school!' One parent from each group felt that at times their child did not concentrate, so that work not completed at school had to be finished at home.

In terms of progress made, ten of the 13 NERs' parents referred to progress in reading. They usually commented on the type of material being read: 'she reads whole books with chapters, smaller print and fewer pictures'; 'he reads more complex books with smaller pictures and more writing on the page'; 'he is more confident and will tackle unknown books'. Parents also made more general comments about reading: 'she understands humour in books better'; 'she is more patient with herself and tries words she doesn't know'; 'he is reading longer books with greater understanding'. Parents of three of the YERs felt that there had been no change in their child's reading and a further five parents commented on progress: four mentioned denser, longer or more grown up texts; two that their children had developed reading stamina and one felt that the child was reading more non-fiction. This may well have been because once word-reading accuracy had become automatic, it was more difficult for the parents to recognise changes.

The parents of 11 YERs and eight NERs referred to progress in writing. This was often in the form of a comment about handwriting: 'writing is smaller and neater now'; 'handwriting is the most significant change'; 'letter formation has improved'. Parents of YERs commented: 'writing is more expressive, with more descriptive words'; 'he writes longer stories with better punctuation'; 'story writing has improved'. Parents of NERs commented: 'structure is clearer and spelling more confident'; 'she writes more independently'; 'he has a go at unknown words'. The parent of one YER felt that there had been little change in her child's writing, and that perhaps there was insufficient encouragement at school.

The parents of five YERs made general comments about their child's progress:

> He has been interested in the topics and keen to follow up history work at home.

> Her philosophical thinking constantly amazes me, her whole world view has expanded.

> She has matured in the way she thinks about things.

> He makes more use of his reading. He comes out with amazing long words he has come across when reading.

> He has grown a huge amount intellectually. He shows his knowledge gained from books and quotes from books.

What parents felt had fostered reading and writing development

Parents found the questions relating to what had fostered their child's reading and writing development at school difficult to answer. Parents were often unable to identify those activities that had enthused their child or had promoted development. This was perhaps particularly true in connection with writing. Parents often made comments like 'she doesn't talk about writing', or simply 'I don't know [what writing they do at school]'. One parent remarked: 'It would be nice to have a little book with her writing in it [sent home from school regularly] so that we could see how she is getting on.'

Reading development

Year R

Of the eight parents of YERs interviewed at the end of YR, one did not know what had fostered her child's continuing reading development; two categorically stated that nothing at school had fostered reading, and one added that the child read more 'grown up' books at home. One parent said that a poetry week had encouraged an interest in poetry and one that a 'book week' had engendered enthusiasm. Two parents felt that having a variety of books, appropriate to their child's level, chosen by the class teacher had helped, and one said that her child enjoyed the reading and listening corners at school. One parent said that changing books every day at school had encouraged the child to read every day, but added that reading was the child's favourite pastime anyway and that 'his reading was so fluent before school'.

The parents of the six NERs also found it hard to answer this question. One felt that the reading scheme used had not encouraged the child, and another said that her child preferred a particular reading scheme to the one that was used. Two parents felt that their child was 'not really reading' and was relying on picture and context clues; one of these parents found 'bringing home the same book for a week . . . increasingly monotonous'. One parent said that reading being part of a routine had helped and added that her child enjoyed choosing books at the library. Another parent said that her child looked for stories she had heard read at school and also looked for information connected with topic work. One parent also mentioned a poetry week, and another a workshop for parents as having been helpful in informing her about what to do at home.

Year 1

Of the parents of the YERs, nine felt that very little had fostered reading development during their child's time in Y1. These children were often given free choice of books and brought home those which their parents thought were not challenging. The YERs did not always read the books brought home from school, and one parent said 'nobody seems to check'. Parents felt that the children, who were after all only 5–6 years old, needed some help when choosing books. Indeed the one parent who was enthusiastic about the guidance her child was receiving at school said that the teacher chose the child's books: 'The teacher knows what her interests are and has said "she needs that extra stimulation".' Three parents said that their child enjoyed going to the school library to research topic work, although they usually did not do this frequently. Books chosen from the school library (and those from home and from local libraries) were described as more likely to meet the children's needs. One parent said that her child had had to do a lot more reading in order to carry out his work. Another thought that her child had been encouraged to use his reading skills, but added that she had had no information about differentiated work.

Parents of five NERs said that 'competition' had encouraged their child to read. This was usually competition with their peers, but also an eagerness to work through the reading scheme. One of these parents said that she did not like the way the school tackled reading; one said that her child sometimes repeatedly brought home the same book; and another that, on her request, the child brought home a supplementary reading book rather than one already read at school. One parent felt that very little had helped the child's reading and, like several other parents of YERs, did not like her child choosing books unaided. One parent said that her child felt frustrated because he read only 2–3 pages at school and then had to wait until the next time he read at school, as reading-scheme books were not brought home. In contrast, three parents felt that bringing reading books home regularly helped. One child enjoyed reading a series of books with the same characters, and another liked to bring home words on cards which she enjoyed making into different sentences. One parent mentioned a book week.

Year 2

In Y2, six of the YERs were regarded as having being given a wider range of books to read; these were often books from the school library, from the 'junior' library or from the teachers' own collections. One child often chose the reference books provided for teachers; and one child had been encouraged to take home the book that the teacher was reading to the class, and had then read more in the same series. These books were seen as more appropriate than the child's class reading book (if one was still being brought home). The children were not usually guided in their choice, but one parent reported that the teacher checked that the book was suitable. Five children did not always read the book brought home from school – one was said to be more likely to take a book from home to read at school, and another child would read about ten books from home to every one school book! Two parents felt that doing comprehension work had helped (including having to cope with 'difficult non-literal' questions), and one parent felt that the amount of reading across the curriculum carried out at school promoted reading skills. One parent said that her child had to keep the school reading book for a week even though it could usually be read by the child at one sitting. Another parent felt her child rarely brought home suitable books and that guided choice would have helped.

Four of the NERs were motivated to read because they wanted to finish the reading scheme and get on to 'free readers'; one of these children also responded well to the comments made in the reading diary. Two parents said that reading regularly helped. One child enjoyed group reading, particularly if the books were humorous, and one had enjoyed diverse reading activities – vocabulary work using dictionaries, comprehension, book reviews and using non-fiction books in relation to topic work. Four parents were unable to say what had fostered reading development: one said that the child did not regularly read books brought home, and another that her child was 'literally left to get on with it'. One child liked reading things to herself at home if she had already read them at school.

Writing development

Year R

Seven parents did not know what had fostered writing development at school. Five parents mentioned handwriting: one felt that handwriting worksheets were not supervised; one that work on letter formation lacked direction; one that a cursive style had initially hindered writing; one that the school seemed to change the style of writing taught; and one that the child had learned a cursive style 'from scratch' at school. One of these parents also said that her child had liked having a personal word book; another parent said that 'having to do it!' had fostered writing development in her (reluctant) writer.

Year 1

Ten parents were unsure about what had fostered writing development in Y1 and two parents felt that nothing had. Some of these parents were aware that their child had to write in different genres – stories, science experiments and news were mentioned. Two parents felt that having to do some writing every day had helped. Ten parents mentioned handwriting practice, including working towards joining, use of finger spaces, writing on and between lines (the latter was said to have helped sizing); one parent felt that her child's letter formation was poor. Another parent knew that her child had learned about capital letters, full stops and speech marks, and one parent said that her child was encouraged to use a dictionary for spelling. Three parents made particular reference to story writing: one that her child had planned stories; another that her child had been able to write longer stories; and the third that a 'fiction book' to write stories in had been beneficial.

138

Year 2

In previous years the parents of the two groups of children had appeared equally lacking in knowledge about the writing that their children did in school. At the end of Y2, the parent of one YER and the parents of seven NERs were either unsure of what had fostered writing development or felt that little had done so; one had remarked that her child 'seems a little bit bored with it all'. Parents of four YERs referred to the amount of writing that their children did – 'It's only this year that they have done any volume' – this perhaps reflecting the fact that writing is physically hard work for young children and that it is only when they start to find writing easier that they are likely to write at length. One YER was said to continue finding writing physically hard. Eight parents mentioned the different genres in which their children wrote; two children were said not to like writing stories, but one child had particularly enjoyed helping to write a book with her class members. Writing stories with chapters was said to have helped fluency in one child. Ten parents mentioned handwriting, usually in relation to the use of a joined/cursive style; two such parents had not liked the use of cursive style earlier on, but were now enthusiastic; however, one parent felt that her child's writing deteriorated when using a joined style and that printing was better. Another parent said that her son 'has seen handwriting as a challenge and is proud of his achievement'. Ten parents mentioned spelling: this group included the parents of four YERs and one NER, all of whom reported that the spellings given to practise at home presented no challenge; one parent said that her child sometimes copied spellings incorrectly and then practised the incorrect version; and one parent said that she would have liked her child to have had more work related to spelling, and that she was also concerned that the child's spelling errors were not pointed out. Only one parent mentioned punctuation, and that was to say that her child was still struggling with apostrophes.

Information from school reports

Parents also received information concerning their children's progress from their school reports and/or Records of Achievement. All but one school produced reports in the Summer Term, and for Y2 children these included their SATs' and Teacher Assessment levels. Some of the reports also included a comment from the child. The information relating to literacy contained in the reports is detailed below. Twelve YR reports (from eight YERs and four NERs), 25 Y1 reports (13 YERs and 11 NERs) and 26 Y2 reports (13 from each group) were examined.

Year R

Seven of the eight YERs' reports commented on their reading ability, usually mentioning fluency, understanding or expression. Comments included:

> Her reading ability is exceptional and she reads with understanding, expression and enjoyment.

> Her brilliant reading skills have enabled her to read to various audiences as well as silently.

> Reading is something he obviously very much enjoys.

All four of the NERs' reports mentioned reading, generally commenting on the good start made with reading or on the building up of sight vocabulary.

The comments about writing indicated that, because of YERs' advanced reading skills, their teachers had high expectations of them in terms of writing, and that these expectations were not always fulfilled:

> He is very careful to try and spell words correctly which takes a long time.

> She knows the sound values of the alphabet and is starting to build up her own words [this child achieved a spelling age of 7.5 years by the second term of YR].

> She needs to be encouraged to 'have a go' before being given the correct spelling.

> She is as yet reluctant to write and this is where she needs to apply herself.

Several teachers commented on handwriting or letter formation. For example: 'Writing has been hampered by poor hand control'; and 'he has agreed that he needs to practise his handwriting as it is rather untidy'. Three of the NERs' reports mentioned handwriting, two referring to letter formation and one to growing confidence in writing.

Year 1

All the reports of the YERs commented on the children's good reading skills. In six of the 13 reports examined reading was described as 'excellent', 'exceptional' or 'of a very high standard'; the remaining seven reports used the terms 'fluent', 'very good' and 'competent'. Comments were also made concerning comprehension, the response to books or the manner in which the child read:

Her understanding of the text is very mature.

Comprehension and research skills are of a high standard.

He gets great pleasure from books (both fiction and non-fiction), responding to them with humour and imagination.

She reads with exceptional expression and intonation.

Several reports referred to the use a child made of his/her reading ability and one report to the importance of providing appropriately for the child's reading skills:

Her excellent reading ability has allowed her individual growth in many other areas and is opening new doors of knowledge to her.

Her exceptional reading skills need to be provided for in the classroom situation.

Of the 11 NERs' reports examined, one referred to the child as 'an excellent reader' and two NERs were said to be reading 'well' and 'very well'. In contrast to the YERs' reports, the strategies used when NERs were reading were mentioned in five reports. For example, one NER was said to make 'use of all the cues available', while another was advised to 'try to tackle unknown words by reading on, looking for meaning in the text and then consider phonic attempts'.

The need to read a wider range of texts was referred to in three reports. One comment indicated that a child needed 'to be encouraged to read non-reading scheme books'; another that the child 'should try to read . . . different types of books as well as fiction'.

Spelling and handwriting were the aspects of writing most frequently mentioned in reports for both groups. Eleven of the 13 YERs' reports referred to spelling. Although the mean spelling age of the group was nearly three years ahead of their chronological age, the comments made did not always reflect this:

She can spell a wide range of common words.

He attempts own spelling.

She needs to work on her spelling.

Spelling of common words is usually accurate and she is now tackling more complex words with increasing success.

141

This last child had achieved a spelling age of just over ten at the chronological age of 5.75 years!

Nine of the 11 reports on NERs referred to spelling, and, while some comments indicated the strategy being used, others were similar to the comments made about the YERs:

> He uses phonic knowledge when spelling.

> Spelling is showing phonological development and she is beginning to remember key irregular words.

> She attempts own spelling with some accuracy.

> He can spell a range of common words accurately.

> He makes very good attempts at spelling commonly used words.

Nine of the YERs' reports and all those of the NERs referred to handwriting. Comments for both groups were similar and usually related to letter formation or joining, although size was also mentioned Handwriting was described as 'neat', 'legible', 'clear'. The use of such terms seems to reflect the influence of the National Curriculum level descriptors.

Specific reference was made to punctuation in only five reports (all for YERs). Two comments referred to the need to remember and to check for punctuation, and two to the use of capital letters and full stops.

Year 2

Thirteen reports from each group were examined at the end of Y2.

Nine of the reports for YERs used the terms 'excellent', 'fluent' or 'very fluent' to describe the children's reading. Four reports referred directly to higher order reading skills or a child's ability to use reference material, and eight reports commented on understanding, including the ability to infer meaning and to understand beyond the literal. One example was: 'His understanding of literature has reached a new depth.' Some reports specified comprehension work, as in the comment: 'Her comprehension work shows her depth of understanding.' However, two reports indicated a need for careful reading of comprehension questions. Four reports mentioned reading aloud with appropriate expression. One example was the remark: 'he is able to use good expression to bring characters and plots to life'.

Of the NERs' reports, one used the term 'excellent', four described reading as 'fluent' and two as 'more fluent'; two reports referred to the ability to use reference material, one to the need to refine higher order reading skills and one to the need to encourage the reading of non-fiction texts.

Seven reports mentioned understanding. Comments included:

Comprehension shows a significant improvement.

She must take time to find out meanings of words she does not know.

He has a good level of comprehension.

Two reports referred to reading aloud with expression and one stated that the child should aim to improve intonation and expression. None of the reports on the YERs referred to decoding, but five of the NERs' reports described the strategies that the child used, or should be encouraged to use, when encountering unknown words.

Comments concerning writing were often detailed and referred to different aspects of the writing process. This reflects the increase in the amount of writing expected and produced during Y2, which in turn possibly reflects both the children's growing confidence and skill with the secretarial aspects of writing and the demands of the National Curriculum.

Spelling was referred to in 11 of the YERs' reports and was described as 'accurate', 'very accurate', 'very good' or 'excellent'. Nine of the NERs' reports referred to spelling, and the comments made were more varied: spelling was described as 'good' and 'accurate most of the time'. Some children were able to spell 'simple words', but needed to refine strategies for more complex vocabulary.

Where handwriting was mentioned (in nine YER reports and eight NER reports) it was usually described as 'neat', 'legible', 'joined'. However, for one child from each group this was indicated as an area where further work was needed.

The use of punctuation was described in 17 reports (nine for YER and eight for NER). Five YERs and three NERs were said to use punctuation 'effectively' or 'accurately'. The remaining nine children were said to be able to use punctuation (full stops and capital letters were the most frequently mentioned), but were inconsistent in its use: the teacher of one YER perceptively remarked: 'He is more than capable of correctly punctuating his written work but regularly neglects to do so. It is clearly irrelevant to him at this time.'

Nearly all the reports referred to the type of vocabulary used, the structure of the writing or its purpose and range, and teachers' comments in these areas reflected the level of writing achieved by both groups of children. For the YERs, comments included:

Varied vocabulary, careful sentence structure and accurate spelling contribute to the quality of her work.

Story writing is well constructed and very imaginative, incorporating different characters to add interest and depth.

Writing is varied and often imaginative, sometimes displaying a dry sense of humour.

Writing is well organised and appropriate to audience and purpose.

For the NERs, comments included:

Creative writing is imaginative and descriptive with well developed story lines.

She thinks carefully about why and for whom she is writing.

Work is imaginative, using an increasing range of vocabulary.

He writes for a variety of purposes and is particularly imaginative.

Three children (one YER and two NERs) were described as at times 'losing the thread' in longer pieces of work, and three NERs were said to need to expand their use of 'descriptive' vocabulary.

Most of the comments in reports reflected the in-depth knowledge that the teachers had acquired of individual children. The majority of the schools presented their reports at the end of the school year, although, as we have seen, parents would have welcomed such information earlier so that they could better support their child's literacy development. Although all the schools had an 'open-door' policy and many parents were happy to initiate discussions, several parents felt that more school-initiated discussions would have been useful. They did not wish to be perceived as 'pushy', and expressed an awareness of the great demands on teachers' time. Parents were generally more knowledgeable about their children's reading than their writing.

8

CHILD INTERVIEWS

In this chapter we report on the interviews that were held with the children towards the end of the project. Semi-structured interviews were carried out in the Summer Term of Y2. By this time the mean age of the children was 7.25 years and we knew the children very well. We were trying to gain a picture of the children's spontaneous reading behaviour and some insight into their attitudes to reading and writing. As will be clear from the responses, when they talked about reading the children were generally referring to reading as a leisure activity, i.e. reading for pleasure.

We asked the children about:

- their current reading and their favourite authors
- where the books read at home came from
- the genre or genres they enjoyed
- whether they read to other people and their attitudes to this type of activity
- where they did most of their reading and writing
- where they most liked to read
- whether they liked writing, or preferred reading to writing, and which they found harder and why
- what they liked doing best.

Current reading

All the YERs at the time of the interviews were reading books from sources other than a reading scheme. Most of the children were reading at least two books – one at home and another at school. Each was able to report the title of the book, or the name of the series if not the individual book title. Two of the children mentioned that they were 'free readers' so were able to choose any books in school.

The less-advanced reading skills of the NERs showed in the books they reported reading. Seven of these children mentioned the colour-code of the book or that it was from a reading scheme, but only two of them did not mention a book title at all. (Many of the schools used a colour-coding system to grade the books into levels of difficulty. This is designed to help the children to choose books that are theoretically within their range of reading ability.)

Listed below are all the responses the children made when asked about their current reading and favourite authors. An 'S' after the title indicates that the book was from school; an 'H' indicates that it was from home. The Oxford Reading Tree scheme books are indicated by 'ORT'.

YERs

- Books from the Junior library (S)
  The Famous Five series (H)
- *The Saddlebag Hero* (S)
  Finders Keepers (H)
- Gold (S)
  The Battle of the Class Clowns
  'Harder books at home' –
  A French puzzle-book
- *Matilda*
  Tales from Toyland
  The Naughtiest Girl is a Monitor
- Chapter books (S)
  Septimouse, Supermouse (H)
  Encyclopedias (H)
  Fairy-tale books (H)
- Paperbacks (S)
  Class One on the Move (S)
  Around the World in Eighty days (H)
- *Railway Cat and Digby* (S)
  Two Village Dinosaurs (H)
- *The Otter Who Wanted to Know* (S)
  The Railway Children (H)
  The Happy Prince & Other Stories (H)
- Mystery stories, like the Famous Five series
- The Narnia series
- Fact and fiction (S)
  Hiccup Harry (S)
  The Dragon in Class 4 (H)

NERs

- Long books
  The Magic Finger (S)
  George's Marvellous Medicine (H)
- Children's novels
  The Little Princess
  'Thick poetry'
- Orange – ORT
  Viking Adventure
- Black
  The Dragon Becomes a Pet (S)
- ORT (S)
  Fireman Sam (H)
- 'Really hard books'
  Quack, Quack, Stick to My Back (S)
- Level 8 Banana Books (S)
- *My Dog Sunday*
- Black (S)
  Goosebumps (H)
- *The Marble Crusher* (S)
- Green (S)
  'Something about space' (H)
- ORT (S)
  Free reader (H)
- Thunderbooks (S)
  Bedtime stories (H)
- *Emily's Legs* (S)
  Dilly the Dinosaur (H)

- *Sing for Your Supper* (S)
  The Magician's Nephew (H)
- *How the World Became and Other
  Stories* (S)
  The Famous Five books (H)
- *Henrietta and the Tooth Fairy*
- *The Wizard of Oz* (S)
  Magic in the Air (H)

When asked 'What are you reading at the moment?', Clarissa chose to answer literally – 'I'm not reading anything at the moment!' She laughed, and went on to detail her current reading.

Henrietta said:

> Paperbacks ('cos I've finished Red-class and Yellow-class books). At school I'm reading *Class One on the Move*. At home *Around the World in Eighty Days*. I've finished *Little Women*, have you ever read it? And I've finished *Alice Through the Looking Glass*.

Bob said:

> Books that are long (sometimes over 100 pages, there's 10 shelves of them). They're like *The Magic Finger*. I've read some things different at home – *George's Marvellous Medicine*. I get Roald Dahl books from school and from the library.

Hope said she was reading

> Really hard books. *Quack, Quack, Stick to My Back* is my school reading book. Mummy's reading *Alice in Wonderland* to me at home.

Mark said:

> At home I read *Goosebumps* – words like 'because' and things, with seven letters or 15. At school I'm nearly on free readers – I read Black stickers.

The respective abilities of the YERs and the NERs was clearly reflected in the level of the books they were reading. Contrast Henrietta who had finished *reading Alice Through the Looking Glass* with Hope who was *listening* to *Alice in Wonderland*.

Favourite author

It will come as no surprise that Roald Dahl was the favourite author of 13 out of the 29 children, although Tamsin said that she only 'quite liked' Roald Dahl and had not really got a favourite author. Clare liked Roald Dahl 'because he makes his stories feel like they're real.'

The favourite authors of each group are listed below, with the number of children mentioning them given in parenthesis. Five of the NERs would not venture a favourite author; some children gave more than one name.

YERs	*NERs*
Roald Dahl (6)	Roald Dahl (7)
Enid Blyton (5)	Dick King-Smith (3)
Dick King-Smith (4)	A. A. Milne (1)
Keith Chatfield (1)	Beatrix Potter (1)
Jill Murphy (1)	
Shirley Hughes (1)	
Oscar Wilde (1)	

Where the books read at home came from

We asked the children where the books they read at home came from: e.g. home, school, libraries, etc. They were all reading books from both home and school, and several regularly read books from libraries. However, when asked where the books *mostly* came from it was interesting to see that the majority of the YERs tended to read mainly their own books, as can be seen from lists below.

YERs	*NERs*
From home (12)	From home (6)
From school (2)	From school (4)
From library (1)	Equally From home and school (1)
	From library (3)

Additional comments from the children revealed their attitudes to some of the books they were required to read. Hope said: 'Home books I usually read, school books I have to read.' Clarissa made a similar comment: 'I'm meant to mostly read my school books, but I don't. I mainly read my own books.'

Kathleen said she mostly read books already at home 'because they're the most grown up.' Two YERs indicated that they were avid readers. Nadine said: 'As long as it's a book I'll read it!' Similarly Tamsin: 'I think I've read almost every book I've ever seen.'

Lynne, however, was enjoying the unusually warm spell of weather at the time of the interview and said: 'Mostly I don't really read books that much – I'm mostly playing outside'!

Genres

The children were asked about the types of book and the other materials that they read. We gave examples of possible answers, such as comics, newspapers and magazines.

All the NERs mentioned reading stories. Three NERs mentioned reading poetry, and six referred to finding-out books (including Lynne who mentioned dictionaries and also said that 'Daddy reads me the encyclopedia'); Fred gave nursery rhymes as an example and Sue said: 'I read picture books, and sometimes I read story books with little black and white pictures in.' Sue also read comics – 'when I run out of books'. Grace, too, referred to comics, saying: 'Sometimes I have comics, but I never read them – I just look for the puzzles.'

In general the YERs reported reading a wider range of genre. They, too, all mentioned reading stories, and often made specific comments about their reading. Benjamin and Gillian referred to the Famous Five series; and Benjamin also liked the Secret Seven; Gillian, however, stated that she did not read Secret Seven books! Others in the group mentioned books of fairy-tales, Young Puffins, paperbacks and chapter books. Kathleen said that she liked story books 'because there's mostly a video that goes with them like *The Railway Children* and *Alice in Wonderland*'.

Tamsin agreed: 'When I've watched TV I look for a book based on the same story.'

Six mentioned reading comics including *Batman*, the *Dandy*, the *Beano* and *Sonic*. Seven referred to finding-out books: Rosalind was reading *What's a Mineral* because she collected stones, and Malcolm said that he mostly read finding-out books with the *Beano* 'second mostly'. Four children mentioned reading magazines: Clarissa and Rosalind specified *Girl Talk*; Rosalind also read *The Brownie* magazine; Jeremy read *Buzz*, and Tamsin said: 'Sometimes I pick Mum's magazine *Woman's Weekly*. I look for the interesting bits.' Three mentioned poetry, and Gillian read the stories that she had written (rather like Disraeli who commented that if he wanted to read a novel he wrote one).

Reading to other people

All but one of the YERs preferred to read to themselves, and seven of them specifically said that they did not like reading to other people. One said she would prefer not to. Most of the children could give reasons, three saying that they could read faster when reading to themselves, and four that it was quieter! Their comments included:

- 'Because I can read it quicker' (Benjamin).
- 'Sometimes I read to my Mummy and [teacher]. I don't like reading to other people as much as I like reading to myself – it's quieter. I don't like to say it out loud – I get all jumbled up when I read it out loud' (Clarissa).
- 'I prefer reading to myself because I can go downstairs and write in my book [home–school diary] "Read to end" and get my Mum to write "Well done"' (Desmond).
- Florence liked reading to others, 'but they sometimes tell me to slow down a bit, I'm a very fast reader'. But she preferred reading to herself, 'because I can read fast and I like reading to myself'.
- 'Well, I read my school reading book aloud to Mummy, Daddy, [brothers] and [teacher] and the people who come in to help [at school]. Other books I read in my head. I like reading in my head because then other people don't hear you. They can get to sleep and when I learnt it I couldn't stop doing it, it just went into my head' (Henrietta).
- 'Sometimes I read to my Mummy and my Daddy and my dog – books about dogs. I read to some of my friends and to [teacher]. I don't really like reading to other people. I like reading to myself in my head – 'cos I can read in peace' (Nadine).
- Jeremy said that he only read out loud 'When other people want me to.' He preferred reading to himself 'so I can have a bit of peace.'
- Gillian preferred reading to others. She said she found it easier, 'because I don't get noises from my [younger] sister'. She added that she didn't read to her sister, 'because I've got to teach her how to skip first'.

The NERs also tended to prefer reading to themselves, although only three stated that they did not like reading to others at all. Four actually preferred reading to others, and the remaining seven children indicated that they quite enjoyed reading to a variety of other people

Unlike the YERs, several of the NERs referred to other people's reactions to their reading and to strategies they employed when reading to themselves.

- 'If I'm reading to someone else, like my sister, she may ask what it means and I can get through it easier if I'm not [reading aloud]' (Bob).
- Although Nan liked reading to others she preferred reading to herself, 'because I don't have to ask for words when I read to myself [she said, laughing, that she missed words out that she didn't know]. She added:

'I don't like my sister reading to me because she doesn't know many words.' Kate also said that she missed words out when she was reading to herself.

- In contrast, Ruth said that she liked reading to others, ''cos if I get my words wrong they can help me out'. Nevertheless, she preferred reading to herself: 'It's more quieter when I read to myself because I can read to myself in my head.'

- Mark, who was something of a philosopher, was in a dilemma: 'The thing is I don't know if I've said the word right or not [when reading to myself]. But I prefer reading to myself because I don't have to bother about them saying, 'No that's not right', or 'You've got to read that over again' – not that that's particularly bad.'!

- Lynne's enjoyment of outside activities was also shown in her answer to this question: 'I like reading to myself, 'cos then you can get it done and you don't have to come in from outside when you're playing a really good game.'

These responses are clearly interesting in the light of National Curriculum assessments. The YERs were at such a level of fluency that reading aloud simply slowed them down. What they wanted was to read *per se*, rather than to practise a skill. Once reading becomes sufficiently fluent, reading aloud moves into a different dimension as a 'declamatory' skill, for which an appreciative audience is required!

Where they did most of their reading and writing

Overwhelmingly, both groups of children judged that they did more reading at home and more writing at school: 13 YERs and 12 NERs said that they read more at home than at school. Two, one child from each group, said they read more at school, and one from each group thought that they read the same amount at home and at school. Here again it must be emphasised that they were taking 'reading' to mean reading for pleasure and not as part of the curriculum. In contrast, for writing, 13 YERs and ten NERs said they wrote more at school; two YERs and 3 NERs said that they wrote more at home, and one NER that it was about equal. A number of the children had for some time written for pleasure, but as the demands of school increased, they found writing to be physically increasingly demanding, as we shall see below.

Very few children elaborated on this question. However, Nadine said: 'I write lots of stories at home, so I'd say I write more at home.' Clare said: 'I've got a big box of paper at home and I take a piece out and start to write a story.' Ruth claimed to 'constantly write poems and stories.'

Preference for place of reading

We asked the children whether they preferred to read at home or at school. Then, additionally, regardless of the preference, we asked where in the home they preferred to read.

Their responses were very clear: most of the children preferred to read at home in bed or in their bedrooms! This replicates the finding of Norris and Stainthorp (1991) and Stainthorp (1994). One can conjure up a lovely picture of the nation's children happily cuddled up in bed reading – not quite what the press would have us believe.

Thirteen YERs and 11 NERs preferred to read at home, with ten YERs and 12 NERs preferring to read in their bedrooms or upstairs. Of the remaining four YERs, three liked to read on the sofa downstairs; one just said 'downstairs' – 'there's a little corner tucked away behind the dining table'; and one in the garden (these interviews were conducted in the Summer Term). One NER also liked to read on the sofa downstairs and one expressed no preference.

The children's comments often referred to comfort, quiet or being able to read for as long as and when they liked.

- 'At home, because I can sit down on the sofa which is nice and comfy. There are hard chairs at school' (Desmond).
- Clarissa, Clare, Grace, Paul and Nan all gave similar reasons for preferring to read at home: 'there aren't as many children' (Clarissa); 'no one can annoy me' (Clare); 'there's not so much noise at home' (Grace); 'at school people go rushing down the corridor when we're supposed to be reading silently' (Paul); 'it's noisy at school and I can't concentrate' (Nan). Nan also liked reading in her bedroom, 'because it's nice and peaceful'.
- Gillian, however, preferred to read at school: 'It's quieter in the quiet reading area – my sister's noisy at home.' Presumably for the same reason her favourite place to read at home was 'out in the garden with the guinea pigs'.
- Nadine liked reading in her bedroom ''cos it's nice and quiet'. Kathleen liked reading upstairs, 'where no one can bother me – in my bedroom, but not always in my bedroom because I share with my sister. On the toilet or on the bathroom floor.'
- Henrietta preferred reading at home where she had more time. Similarly, Sue said: 'I like reading when I come back from school 'cos then I can read for a long time.' Hope liked reading at home, 'because I can read when I like'. Phillip, however, preferred to read at school, 'because at school you can read as long as you like because it's not "nearly bedtime"'.
- Two children gave somewhat different reasons for their choice: Shelagh

preferred reading at home ''cos I've got better books'; and Mark at school, because 'you have more people to read to'.

Writing

Although only Desmond, Bob and Lynne said that they did not like writing, several other children qualified their responses. Jeremy, Benjamin, Malcolm, Kate and Paul liked writing stories but did not like other types of writing. 'I don't like practising handwriting because I can already do it' (Benjamin); 'I don't like writing about sums' (Paul). Henrietta too did not like handwriting: 'First you have to wait for people and you can't do the whole sheet in one go. I don't mind doing a little bit of writing – like a card – I like it then.' Joe liked writing but had not enjoyed his recently completed SAT writing task 'It took too long.'

The YERs, unsurprisingly in view of the ease with which they had acquired their reading skill, preferred reading to writing, and also found it easier than writing. Jeremy and Clare were unable to say which they preferred. Kathleen said that she found both 'too easy', and Clare and Paul were unable to say which they found the harder, Clare said: 'If you don't know how to read a word it's the same as not knowing how to write a word.'

Of the children who could decide, 11 YERs and eight NERs preferred reading to writing. Only two YERs but six NERs found reading harder than writing.

Six of the YERs cited spelling as the reason for finding writing harder, despite the fact that their spelling skills were considerably in advance of their chronological ages. Gillian said: 'You have to guess how to spell words.' Nadine offered: 'There might be some words you can't spell – hard words.'

Four of the YER group said that writing made their hands or arms ache. Phillip said 'Your arms get aching [when you write], your arms don't ache holding a book.' Desmond said: 'All you do is sit and write, and when you've wrote a lot your hand aches.'

The only NER to directly state that writing made his hand ache was Bob, although both Lynne and Mark referred to the length of time that it took them to write. Lynne said 'I don't like doing writing very much, it takes a long time to write a story.' Both Bob and Mark found aspects of hand-writing difficult: Bob said that he sometimes forgot to join his writing and that he crossed out a lot; and Mark that he found it hard to remember both the upper- and lower-case forms of letters. Don and Hope found reading harder because they could not miss words out, whereas in writing they could just 'have a go'. Kate, conversely, found writing harder because she felt that she couldn't miss words out in writing, but she could when reading. Only Ruth referred directly to spelling: ''cos if you don't know how to spell a word it's hard'.

Malcolm was the only child from either group who said that he found writing harder because it was difficult to think what to write, although his Y2 teacher's comment indicated that he was a very successful writer: 'he has written remarkable poems and stories. He has a maturity of understanding and extensive vocabulary which he incorporates into his work.'

Preferred pastime

The children were asked what they would do if they could choose anything; they were then asked if their chosen activity was better than reading. Obviously these answers may be a little suspect because there was a degree of wanting to please by giving the answer they thought might be expected! However, the children were remarkably frank, although they found it a difficult question to answer. For example, Tamsin said: 'I like all sorts of things. I really, really, really enjoy reading and playing and watching TV.'

Of the YERs

- five said they would read, but that it was equal to watching TV or swimming or going to the park;
- five said they would draw (pictures, maps, charts and colouring were mentioned), four of these children claiming their chosen activity to be better than reading.

The remaining YER children, too, all thought their chosen activity was better than reading, each giving one of the following:

- playing cricket or carry out activities with his parents
- playing the keyboard (she had moved onto this from the piano)
- going to Chessington World of Adventure or Legoland
- playing football
- either gym or playing with plasticene.

The NERs gave similar responses:

- Three liked reading best. Clare, for example, said: 'I've got lots of favourite things – to buy tons of books, to go on holiday round the world and to have all the money in the world. I like losing myself in a book. I like silence 'cos I can imagine it.'
- Three said they would play football – two thought that it was better than reading. Paul commented: 'I'm not sure it's my favourite but it's much better than reading.' However, Mark added this philosophical thought: 'I love football. It's not really better than reading, 'cos I know that if I read I'll get a better view of things and do better in my exams.'

- Three said they would go swimming, two ranking it equal with reading. Sue said: 'It's not better than reading because I get cold in the swimming pool.'
- One said she would play on the computer which she thought was the same as reading in terms of interest.

Each of the remaining children thought that his/her chosen activity was better than reading:

- TV and going out to dinner or to see a film
- art work
- writing
- playing out.

All in all a very normal, lively, bunch of children – to whom we are most grateful for all their personal time and insights.

Although for many of the children reading and learning to read were primarily means to some end, others indicated a more personal focus on reading itself. This is perhaps best illustrated by Clare's comment, above, and also by Kathleen, who said: 'Nobody bothers me. They think, "She's stuck in a book, I'll just leave her there".'

9

LEARNING FROM SUCCESSFUL READERS

Introduction

In this chapter we consider how the data collected in this study relate to current theories of literacy development. The importance of the 'Matthew effect' is discussed and group similarities and differences explored. Finally, we consider educational implications.

What made these children successful?

This question relates both to the YERs and to the NERs. The NERs were all doing very well, and most of them found it relatively easy to learn to read once they began to receive formal reading instruction. The YERs were quite simply exceptional. This word can be used here without a hint of hyperbole.

The preschool experiences of all the children were major contributory factors. Their home backgrounds were varied and by no means could they be generally described as privileged. However, the parental questionnaires and interviews showed that the parents were providing the sort of environment known to be influential in fostering receptiveness to literacy. Print was a strong feature in the homes: parents and other adults read to the children from an early age, regularly and from a variety of materials. The library was also something that featured regularly in the children's lives. Their encounters with books ensured that the children were familiar with discursive styles of writing, albeit in storybook language. This also meant that they had extensive acquanitance with the story form – introduction, development, resolution. These early encounters with texts seem to put children at an advantage when they begin to learn to read.

The questionnaire data given by the parents at the beginning of the project would suggest that attitudes towards reading and books were not just assumed to encourage the children. The parents themselves had positive personal attitudes, which they modelled for their children either deliberately or subconsciously.

These attitudes did not relate just to reading. There was plenty of writing

156

activity going on in the homes, including use of computers. The children had opportunities to internalise the uses of literacy in a very prosaic but potent way. So many of the parents described themselves as avid list-makers. The list is an important example of writing for a purpose, and one which is concrete and meaningful in the mind of a child. Writing lists is a behaviour which is easy to imitate.

Knowledge of the alphabet is one of the most important achievements in relation to the early acquisition of literacy, and the parental reports show that the children had many opportunities for learning their letters. By the time they started school, the YERs had almost complete alphabetic knowledge, whereas the NERs did not. However, the NER group members had sufficient knowledge to enable them to begin to use decoding strategies early on in their literacy development.

All the parents were providing an appropriately literate rich environment for their children, but clearly there were quite dramatic differences in terms of skill acquisition between the two groups when we started the study. The activities engaged in by both sets of families were similar, but the outcomes were very different. The YERs had been able to capitalise on these experiences and teach themselves to read, whereas the NERs could be considered to have stored up the experiences so that they were primed and ready to start learning to read when they began to receive systematic instruction in school. At that point they, too, were able to capitalise on their experiences, and so made rapid progress in school.

It was quite clear from the parental questionnaires that the YERs were the pacemakers in literacy activities in the home. They were not forced by their parents to read, but their own developing skills indicated that they were interested in literacy activities and they therefore deliberately engaged in more of them. This is a strong demonstration of positive Matthew effects. The individuals' interest and ability ensured that they chose to engage in literacy activities, which in turn meant that they were improving these skills all the time.

Our data on phonological sensitivity shed light on the individual differences. The pairs of individuals in the two groups had been matched on receptive vocabulary development. This meant that there was greater variability *within* than there was *between* the groups. However, the difference between the two groups, when we tested their phonological sensitivity at five years, was dramatic. The YERs were not at ceiling on these tasks but they were clearly able to do them with some degree of success. On the other hand, the NERs were able to provide and detect rhyme, but could do none of the other tasks with comparable success.

Their performance on nonword reading showed just how well the YERs were able to decode words. It is not enough to be phonologically sensitive and to know the alphabet – it is essential that children are able to integrate this knowledge and use it to construct plausible phonological candidates for unknown words.

In terms of scripting, there were no differences in the groups' handwriting skills – both groups found handwriting initially physically demanding. However, because the YERs had advanced spelling skills they had more processing capacity available for compositional aspects of writing. They did not write at greater length, but in their simple sentences there were fewer redundancies and ambiguities and they attempted more complex structures in their writing than did the NERs.

Current theories about reading and writing development

There may not be absolute consensus among psychologists about the processes that are involved in reading and writing development, but people seem to agree about some things. One is that in order to read and write in an alphabetic system children need to have good knowledge of the letters of the alphabet. This means being able to discriminate letters visually, naming them, and knowing the phonemes they most commonly represent. They also need to be sensitive to the phonemic structure of words and capable eventually of manipulating the phonemes, thus differentiating sound from semantics. They need to be able to combine this knowledge so that they can map letter–sound correspondences. In addition they need to be able to use this knowledge to decode unknown written words and so to access phonologies. This means they must be able to map letters onto sounds and then blend the resultant phoneme sequence. When spelling, they need to be able to segment their chosen word into a sequence of phonemes, converting them into a sequence of graphemes, which they then produce in the correct sequence.

In addition to this sublexical route for reading and spelling, some models propose that children also develop a direct route for reading and spelling which involves the development of a visual lexicon. Through decoding and recoding words, permanent descriptions of words are built up which means that words can be recognised complete, without the need for utilising the output from the sublexical route. Multiple exposure to visual words and their (correctly produced) phonologies ensures that their orthographic identities are represented on the lexicon.

Multiple exposure also means that children become aware of the patterns that make up much of orthography, and so capitalise on their awareness in order to reduce the workload when tackling new and unknown words. Under such circumstances they may well be able to use an analogy strategy to go from a known to an unknown word.

The performance of the children in our study acts as an exemplification of these models of reading and spelling development. The YERs had almost perfect knowledge of the alphabet at the start of the study *and* were able to manipulate the sounds in words with great success. The evidence we obtained suggested that alphabetical knowledge and ability to manipulate sounds were integrated and available for use as a means of tackling unknown words. Thus the YER children had high levels of skill at reading nonwords. At the start of the study the NERs had reasonable levels of alphabet knowledge and they could rhyme, but they had only limited phonological sensitivity beyond rhyming and therefore insufficient knowledge to read successfully. As they gained phonological sensitivity, they began to read words and nonwords. Mapping their performance against that of the YERs, it would seem that phonological sensitivity preceded word reading in the main. However, both groups of children found segmenting words into phonemes a challenging task. We could speculate that, initially, the YERs' spelling skills lagged behind their reading skills because they found segmentation more difficult than other phonological tasks. By the age of six they were able to use their lexical knowledge when spelling both words and nonwords. Nevertheless, their spelling skills remained less developed than their reading skills. This is probably because it is possible to read a word when it is only partially specified in the lexicon, but complete representation is necessary in order to spell it. Thus we might read both *said* and *siad* as 'said', but we would be able to spell it correctly only if we had the correct lexical representation. Evidence from the NERs showed that early spelling relied on segmentation and application of letter–sound correspondences. It is, however, difficult to determine at what stage in development spelling can be said to be lexically mediated. Snowling (1994) suggested that neither lexical nor sublexical strategies work in isolation, although dual-route models imply such independence.

'Matthew effects'

The project has shown just how important positive Matthew effects are in education. The YERs were able to read with relative ease and as a result could concentrate on the content of their reading rather than the processing of the words themselves. The teachers were very clear that the general knowledge of the YERs was considerably enhanced by their independent reading. The children's own self reports about their leisure reading show how their ability meant they were reading more. Their exposure to print was very high. They may not have spent more time reading, although they generally enjoyed the activity, but their advanced reading automaticity and reading speed meant that they were able to process considerably more print in the same period of time as did children with less advanced skill. Not only that, but because they were able to process the print so easily it took up far less of their processing capacity, leaving them with more capacity to focus on the meaning of texts. They were able also to use knowledge gained from

159

their reading when writing. They used spelling strategies, punctuation and structures in their writing that they had not been taught, having formulated their own hypotheses from their exposure to print.

There is one aspect of the YERs' development which is curious and warrants further investigation: vocabulary development. The two groups of children were very carefully matched on the British Picture Vocabulary Scale (BPVS) at the beginning of the study. There was variability *within* but no significant difference *between* the groups, and all the children were scoring above a percentile of 50. It was very important that the two groups were matched, otherwise it could have been that the YERs were better readers because of higher general ability (the BPVS correlates highly with verbal IQ). We decided to retest all the children at the end of the study, because we wanted to see whether advanced reading had any consequences for vocabulary.

The results of this end-of-study test suggest that there had been very little change in percentile rankings and no significant difference between the two groups. The YERs scored slightly higher, but not significantly so. This suggests that our matching had indeed been rigorous, but it is perplexing in relation to the possible consequences of literacy. The YERs who were so much more widely read had not increased their receptive vocabulary any more than had the NERs. There was some anecdotal evidence about spoken vocabulary effects: children sometimes used words appropriately but with incorrect pronunciation, indicating that they had encountered such words only in their own reading. For example, Jeremy knew that a mosquito was 'a little insect' but read it as /mɒ skwɪt əʊ/; Tamsin correctly used the words sabotage, stingy, quay and debris but pronounced them as /sæbə teɪʤ /, /stɪŋ ɪ/, /kweɪ/ and /debrɪs/. When asked how she knew what something meant, Tamsin often said that she had read it. Nevertheless, there were no overall effects on vocabulary – this is a paradox. One explanation is that the NERs were bright and being read to at home and at school. Indeed there was evidence that parents were reading to the NERs similar books to those that the YERs themselves were reading. In addition, some teachers reported raising the level of vocabulary (and language generally) that they used in the classroom because of the input from the YERs.

Educational implications

Schools have to provide an appropriately challenging diet for all pupils. It is part of the philosophy of the British education system that as many children as possible should be educated in mainstream schools. A driving tenet is integration of children with special educational needs. Realistically, issues about recognition and provision for children with special educational needs revolve round children who have learning difficulties or motor or perceptual difficulties. Nevertheless, children who have exceptional abilities have in the past been included among those considered to have special educational needs. One child in this study was given an Individual Educational Plan because the school was concerned to ensure that she was given a curriculum challenging enough to capitalise on her advanced literacy skills.

Questions are beginning to be asked about provision for children who might variously be described as 'able', 'exceptionally able', 'gifted' or 'talented'. Detailed discussion is beyond the scope of this book. However, with the advent of the national literacy *Framework for Teaching* (DfEE 1998), the evidence provided here does have implications for teaching. The 'literacy hour' is predicated mainly on whole-class teaching, with some small-group teaching. During the whole-class sessions the less-able children are expected to gain from observing and modelling the performance of the more able. This may well work when the whole class is fairly close in skill development. It would seem to be much more problematic when the occasional child has skills which are significantly in advance of those of the rest. Once all KS1 schools are conducting Baseline Assessments it will become easier to detect a child with advanced literacy skills in the new intake. Under those circumstances considerable thought will have to be given to the choice of teaching group for such a child.

The framework document (DfEE 1998) lays down term-by-term teaching for word-, sentence- and text-level work. The three strands are designed to be taught in a complementary programme in which reading and writing are integrated. Our evidence shows that at the beginning of the study the YERs word-level skills were at least at Y2 level, and in some instances at Y3 level. The 'Matthew effects' of their advanced reading meant that their needs would not be met by reiterating knowledge they had already achieved by themselves, but they did need specific supportive guidance to ensure that they engaged with a wide variety of genres – particularly non-fiction. As the framework makes satisfactorily clear, children have to be taught the skills necessary for reading non-fiction, and for analysing and deconstructing texts of all types. These are very different skills from word-reading skills, and just because children can effectively teach themselves to read words and under-stand texts does not mean that they can independently acquire the necessary skills for advanced engagement with different genres. The best practices we have found acknowledge the need for such teaching, and teachers effectively devise individualised mini-programmes which give the children guidance, for example, on using the library and developing their own study skills, at the time when their peers were learning to become skilled readers. Such in-class solutions are effective because these very young children are supported in an environment with their peers.

It was not always easy for teachers to find appropriate reading materials; material from reading schemes at the YERs' level was often not appropriate in terms of content. We have seen that teachers supplemented books from school with books from their own collections and some also found children's classics suitable: certainly the YERs reported reading books by Lewis Carroll, E. E. Nesbitt and C. S. Lewis. Teachers were careful to monitor comprehension of texts read, although for the YERs this was not a problem; in fact, they displayed the knowledge they had obtained from their own reading in tackling these works. Where schools operated a vertical grouping system of Y1–Y2 classes, in Y1 the YERs were easily slotted into work with the Y2 children and were often said to be functioning at the upper end of the ability range. This became somewhat problematic when they were in Y2. The children needed differentiation of activities, not just differentiation by outcome. This was particularly important for YERs, as outcome was often in written work and we knew that their writing skills often did not reflect their reading ability.

Although at the beginning of the study the YERs were able to write the appropriate letter when a letter name or sound was given, their letter-formation and handwriting skills were no different from those of their peers. They needed the same practice with these skills and found writing as physically demanding as did other children. Nevertheless, they were able to incorporate in their writing hypotheses they had formulated from their reading. Several teachers recognised that although their YER did not necessarily produce more writing, what was written was often more complex.

We have already seen that some automaticity in secretarial skills is necessary in order to free sufficient processing capacity for composition. In the early stages, the children in this study viewed their main problem as not what to write but how to write it. However, we also know that controlled practice of writing leads to improved performance (the Matthew effect). We, therefore, need to consider how best to support continuous writing while children gain mastery of the secretarial aspects (spelling and handwriting in particular). The National Literacy Strategy, alongside word- and sentence-level work, suggests that for text-level work in YR the retelling of familiar stories is one means of supporting writing. The use of patterned stories as models, building profiles of characters from stories read and representing outlines of story plots are also mentioned. In Y1, it is suggested that children substitute and extend patterns from their reading and use elements of known stories to structure their own writing; and, for non-fiction, that they use as models the language of texts read.

The National Literacy Strategy states that children should learn to read as writers, i.e. they need to be able to evaluate critically what they are reading and to identify how successful writers have achieved the desired audience response (in both fiction and non-fiction). The YERs in particular were using information gained from their reading to enhance their writing. They were forming their own hypotheses concerning spelling, structure, punctuation and style. However, this information was not yet articulated, and it must be remembered that their reading ages were significantly in advance of their chronological ages. The NERs were less likely to formulate their own hypotheses. This indicates that reading skills need to be well established before children are able themselves to use knowledge gained from their reading to enhance their writing. However, the texts that children are reading could be used by teachers to exemplify *specific* points concerning writing; that is, this knowledge could be made explicit. Children also need to learn how to write as readers. We have seen from this study that young children find it difficult to monitor their own work for spelling, punctuation and stylistic errors; they are likely to read their work as if it were correct and may be unable to change spelling errors even when they recognise them.

The teachers in this study recognised that planning, drafting and editing were difficult for the children, and it was usually only the 'top' groups in Y2 classes which were involved in these activities, and not always successfully. Comments made by the Y2 teachers, towards the end of the study, reflected this:

The children don't want to do it.

Their drafting is superficial. The children don't want to do it again and haven't got the idea of short plans.

The brighter five or six children are beginning to understand that you don't have to write it all out when planning.

It would kill them off to write twice!

Nevertheless, seven YERs and one NER were awarded levels 3 or 4 in the SATs carried out at the end of KS1. That is, they were deemed to be functioning like children in KS2 and should, therefore, have undertaken planning, drafting and editing as described in the programmes of study for KS2 (DfE 1995: 15) and in the National Literacy Strategy: 'Through Key Stage 2, there is a progressive emphasis on the skills of planning, drafting, revising, proof reading and presentation of writing' (DfEE 1998: 5).

We need to consider why such young children appear to have difficulty with planning, even though they may have been able to cope with the tasks cognitively. There is evidence that some of the children found the physical act of writing both difficult and tiring and they simply did not want to prolong the agony. The lack of all but superficial changes made to spelling, style, handwriting or punctuation reflects their reluctance to rewrite, but may also indicate that in the developing system the correct/incorrect dichotomy is unstable and therefore hard for children to monitor.

If we take handwriting to be not only the production of the written traces but also the retrieval of the appropriate graphemes then we can see the link between handwriting and written spelling. Children may be able to spell a word orally, but unless they can retrieve the correct graphemic motor representation they will be unable to produce the word in written form. For similar letters the graphemic motor pattern is likely to be unstable and to require considerably more practice, with feedback, in order to gain automaticity than is the case for dissimilar letters. Upper- and lower-case allographs may require a similar amount of practice, though here there is the additional problem that the punctuation rules governing their use also have to be learned.

All the schools recognised the important and continuing role that parents have in the development of literacy, and all wished to promote positive home–school links. Parents would have welcomed more school-initiated contact, but they were increasingly aware of the demands on teachers' time and did not wish to add to the burden. Some of the parents were happy to initiate contact with the school from the time their child started there. Others became more confident about approaching school as their child entered Y1 or Y2. In contrast, there were some parents who felt that their contact with their child's school had made little difference to his or her programme of study.

General information concerning reading and writing is often presented when a child starts school and is, therefore, not always immediately relevant. (In addition, such information is easily mislaid!) The parents in this study would have welcomed further information as their children made progress in reading and writing. Several schools provided this in the form of meetings at the beginning of the school year when programmes for the year were discussed. However, parents still felt that information specific to their child would have been helpful. Reports issued at the end of the school year reflected the in-depth knowledge that teachers had of individual children. Many parents would have preferred the information earlier, so that they could better support their children's literacy development. Certainly the parents of children attending the school where formative reports were issued and discussed in the Spring Term were pleased with this approach.

The parents of the YERs were often unable to say which of the activities at school had promoted reading skills. From interviews with the teachers, it was apparent that work on higher order reading skills was being carried out in their schools, but the parents seemed unaware of this. Whereas progress in the early stages of reading can be seen to take place as children bring home increasingly complex texts, this is not necessarily so for the development of higher order reading skills. Teachers need to make explicit the type of work being carried out at school in relation to these skills.

Conclusion

The performance of the children in this study confirmed the importance of and the interrelationship between alphabetic knowledge and phonological skills when learning to read. In addition, all the children experienced print within the home environment from an early age, although the types of experience were diverse. Undoubtedly, sharing appropriate books with interested adults is important; but exposure to print in other forms – papers, magazines, comics, on television and observing people writing – is equally important.

It must be recognised that these positive early experiences are not themselves usually sufficient to enable children to become readers. The YERs seem to have been able to discover for themselves the connections between spoken language and print. Evidence from this study suggests that their superior phonological sensitivity and alphabetic knowledge were instrumental in enabling them to make these connections. Nevertheless, the overwhelming majority of children need direct tuition.

Of course, the question we cannot answer is how the YERs came to have these precocious abilities.

When the study ended it was apparent that not all the YERs had become avid recreational readers, although all made extensive use of their reading skills both at home and at school. Nevertheless, for some, reading had become a source of great pleasure. As Tamsin said:

> I like reading because I can just sort of drift off into a little world of my own and ignore everything around me.

APPENDIX

The phonemes (sounds) of English

Consonant sounds		Vowel sounds	
p	peg	i	tree
b	bad	ɪ	sit
t	tip	e	wet
d	dog	æ	cat
k	king	ɑ	father
g	goat	ɒ	plot
f	fish	ɔ	saw
v	vase	ʊ	put
θ	thumb	u	shoe
ð	they	ʌ	duck
s	soon	ɜ	girl
z	zoo	ə	banana
ʃ	shop	eɪ	play
ʒ	treasure	əʊ	go
ʧ	chip	ai	sigh
ʤ	jug	aʊ	now
m	milk	ɔɪ	boy
n	nice	ɪə	here
ŋ	sing	ɛə	there
l	leg	ʊə	pure
r	red		
j	yellow		
w	watch		
h	house		

BIBLIOGRAPHY

Alston, J. and Taylor, J. (1988) *The Handwriting File, 2nd edn*, Wisbech: Learning Development Aids.

Anderson, H. (1996) 'Vicki's story: A seven year old's use and understanding of punctuation', in N. Hall and A. Robinson (eds), *Learning about Punctuation*, Clevedon: Multilingual Matters.

Baker, C. D. and Freebody, P. (1989) *Children's First School Books*, Oxford: Blackwell.

Barry, C. and Seymour, P. H. K. (1988) 'Lexical priming and sound-to-spelling contingency effects in non-word spelling', *Quarterly Journal of Experimental Psychology* 40A: 5–40.

Beard, R. (1994) 'The writing process', in D. Wray and J. Medwell (eds), *Teaching Primary English*, London: Routledge.

Bradley, L. and Bryant, P. E. (1983) 'Categorising sounds and learning to read: a causal connection', *Nature* 301: 419–21.

Bruce, D. J. (1964) 'The analysis of word sounds by young children', *British Journal of Educational Psychology* 34: 158–70.

Bruck, M. and Waters, G. (1988) 'An analysis of the spelling errors of children who differ in their reading and spelling skills', *Applied Psycholinguistics* 9: 77–92.

Bryant, P. E. and Bradley, L. (1980) 'Why children sometimes write words which they do not read', in U. Frith (ed.), *Cognitive Processes in Spelling*, London: Academic Press.

Bryant, P. E., Devine, M., Ledward, A. and Nunes, T. (1997) 'Spelling with apostrophes and understanding possession', *British Journal of Educational Psychology* 67: 91–110.

Bryant, P. E. and Nunes, T. (1997) 'Spelling and grammar', *Integrating Research and Practice in Literacy: An International Symposium*, London: Institute of Education.

Byrne, B., Fielding-Barnsley, R. and Ashley, L. (1996) 'What does the child bring to the task of learning to read? A summary of the New England reading acquisition projects', *Australian Journal of Psychology* 48(3): 119–27.

Cazden, C. B., Cordeiro, P. and Giacobbe, M. E. (1985) 'Spontaneous and scientific concepts: young children's learning of punctuation', in G. Wells and J. Nicholls (eds), *Language and Learning: An International Perspective*, London: Falmer Press.

Cipielewski, J. and Stanovich, K. (1992) 'Predicting growth in reading ability from children's growth in print', *Reading Research Quarterly* 27: 74–89.

Clark, M. (1976) *Young fluent readers*, London: Heinemann Educational Books.

Clay, M. (1970) *Reading: The Patterning of Complex Behaviour*, Auckland (NZ): Heinemann.

Clay, M. (1993) *An Observational Survey of Early Literacy Achievement*, Auckland (NZ): Heinemann.

Clay, M. M. (1975) *What Did I Write?* Auckland (NZ): Heinemann.

Clay, M. M. (1979) *Sand: The Concepts about Print Test*, Auckland (NZ): Heinemann.

Clay, M. M. (1985) *The Early Detection of Reading Difficulties*, 3rd edn, Auckland (NZ): Heinemann.

Coltheart, M., Davelaar, E., Jonasson, J. and Besner, D. (1977) 'Access to the internal lexicon', in S. Dornic (ed.), *Attention and Performance VI*, Hillsdale, NJ: Lawrence Erlbaum Associates.

De Goes, C. and Martlew, M. (1983) 'Young children's approach to literacy', in M. Martlew (ed.), *The Psychology of Written Language*, Chichester: John Wiley & Sons.

DES (1989) *English in the National Curriculum*, London: HMSO.

DfE (1995) *Key Stages 1 and 2 of the National Curriculum*, London: HMSO.

DfEE (1996) *Teachers' Handbook: English Tasks 1997*, London: HMSO.

DfEE (1998) *National Literacy Strategy: A Framework for Teaching*, London: HMSO.

Dixon, M. (1997) Personal communication.

Dunn, L. M., Dunn, L. M., Whetton, C. and Pintilie, D. (1982) *The British Picture Vocabulary Scale*, Windsor: NFER-Nelson.

Ehri, L.C. (1995) 'Phases of development in learning to read words by sight', *Journal of Research in Reading*, 18(2): 116–25.

Ehri, L. C. (1997) 'Learning to read and learning to spell are one and the same, almost', in C. Perfetti, L. Rieben and M. Fayol (eds), *Learning to Spell: Research, Theory and Practice Across Languages*, London: Lawrence Erlbaum Associates.

Elliot, C. D. (1992) *British Ability Scales: Spelling scale*, Windsor NFER-Nelson.

Elliot, C. D., Murray, D. J. and Pearson, L. S. (1983) *The British Ability Scales*, Windsor: NFER-Nelson.

Ellis, A. W. (1993) *Reading, Writing and Dyslexia: A Cognitive Analysis*, 2nd edn, Hove: Lawrence Erlbaum Associates.

Fredrickson, N. (1995) *Phonological Assessment Battery*, London: University College.

Frith, U. (1985) 'Beneath the surface of developmental dyslexia', in K. E. Patterson, J. C. Marshall and M. Coltheart (eds), *Surface Dyslexia: Neuropsychological and Cognitive Studies of Phonological Reading*, Hillsdale, NJ: Lawrence Erlbaum Associates.

Funnell, E. (1992) 'On recognising misspelled words', in C. M. Robson and C. Sterling (eds), *Psychology, Spelling and Education*, Clevedon: Multilingual Matters.

Gentry, J. R. (1987) *Spel . . . Is a Four Letter Word*, Ontario: Scholastic Canada.

Gimson, A. C. (1962) *An Introduction to the Pronunciation of English*, London: Edward Arnold.

Gombert, J. E., Bryant, P. and Warrick, N. (1997) 'Children's use of analogy in learning to read and spell', in C. Perfetti, L. Rieben and M. Fayol (eds),

Learning to Spell: Research, Theory and Practice Across Languages, London: Lawrence Erlbaum Associates.

Goswami, U. (1991) 'Learning about spelling sequences: the role of onset and rime in analogies in reading', *Child Development* 62: 1110–23.

Gough, P. B., Juel, C. and Griffith, P. L. (1992) 'Reading, spelling and the orthographic cipher', in P. B. Gough, L. C. Ehri and R. Treiman (eds), *Reading Acquisition*, Hillsdale, NJ: Lawrence Erlbaum Associates.

Graves, D. (1983) *Writing: Children and Teachers at Work*, Exeter, NH: Heinemann.

Haines, C. (1996) 'Capital letters: are they an alphabet of difficulties for young children?', *Handwriting Review* 10: 29–39.

Hall, N. and Robinson, A. (eds) (1996) *Learning about Punctuation*, Clevedon: Multilingual Matters.

Hughes, D. (1995) 'The handwriting skills of young early readers', *Handwriting Review* 9: 50–67.

Hughes, D. (1996) 'The handwriting skills of young early readers: one year on', *Handwriting Review* 10: 40–54.

Hughes, D. (1997) 'A longitudinal study of the handwriting skills of children between the ages of 5 and 7 years', *Handwriting Review* 11: 26–47.

Just, M. A. and Carpenter, P. A. (1987) *The Psychology of Reading and Language Comprehension*, Boston, MA: Allyn & Bacon.

Kinmont, A. (1990) *The Dimensions of Writing*, London: David Fulton.

Kress, G. (1994) *Learning to Write*, 2nd edn, London: Routledge.

Kroll, B. M. (1981) 'Developmental relationships between speaking and writing', in B. M. Kroll and R. J. Vann (eds), *Exploring Speaking – Writing Relationships: Connections and Contrasts*, Urbana, IL: National Council of Teachers of English.

Ladefoged, P. (1982) *A Course in Phonetics*, London: Harcourt, Brace and Jovanovich.

Laszlo, J. and Bairstow, P. (1983) 'Kinaesthesis: its measurement, training and relationship to motor control', *Quarterly Journal of Experimental Psychology* 35A: 411–21.

Lennox, C. and Siegel, L. (1996) 'The development of phonological rules and visual strategies in average and poor spellers', *Journal of Experimental Child Psychology* 62: 60–83.

Martens, P. and Goodman, Y. (1996) 'Invented punctuation', in N. Hall and A. Robinson (eds), *Learning about Punctuation*, Clevedon: Multilingual Matters.

McBride-Chang, C. (1995) 'What is phonological awareness?', *Journal of Educational Psychology* 87: 179–92.

Meek, M. (1991) *On Being Literate*, London: Bodley Head.

Morton, J. (1968) *Grammar and Computation in Language Behaviour: Progress Report No. 6*, Ann Arbor: Centre for Research in Language and Language Behaviour, University of Michigan.

Neale, M. D. (1989) *Neale Analysis of Reading Ability – Revised British Edition*, Windsor: NFER-Nelson.

Norris, E. and Stainthorp, R. (1991) 'Reading tuition by elder siblings', *Reading* 25: 13–18.

Nunes, T., Bryant, P. and Bindman, M. (1997) 'Spelling and grammar – the necsed move', in C. A. Perfetti, L. Ruben and M. Fayol (eds), *Learning to Spell: Research, Theory and Practice across Languages*, Mahwah, NJ: Lawrence Erlbaum Associates.

Perera, K. (1984) *Children's Writing and Reading*, Oxford: Blackwell.

Perfetti, C. A., Bell, I. L., Beck, L. C. and Hughes, C. (1987) 'Phonemic knowledge and learning to read are reciprocal: a longitudinal study of first-grade children', *Merrill-Palmer Quarterly* 33: 283–319.

Read, C. (1983) 'Orthography', in M. Martlew (ed.), *The Psychology of Written Language*, Chichester: John Wiley & Sons.

Robinson, A. (1996) 'Conversations with teachers about punctuation', in N. Hall and A. Robinson (eds), *Learning about Punctuation*, Clevedon: Multilingual Matters.

Sassoon, R. (1983) *The Practical Guide to Children's Handwriting*, London: Thames & Hudson.

Sassoon, R. (1993) 'Handwriting', in R. Beard (ed.), *Teaching Literacy and Balancing Perspectives*, London: Hodder & Stoughton.

Sassoon, R. (1994) 'A decade and a half in handwriting', *Handwriting Review 1995*, pp. 53–60.

Scardamalia, M. (1981) 'How children cope with the cognitive demands of writing', in C. H. Frederiksen and J. F. Dominic (eds), *Writing: The Nature, Development and Teaching of Written Communication*, Hillsdale, NJ: Lawrence Erlbaum Associates.

Seidenberg, M. S. and McClelland, J. L. (1989) 'A distributed developmental model of word recognition and naming', *Psychological Review* 96: 523–68.

Seymour, P. H. K. and Elder, L. (1986) 'Beginning reading without phonology', *Cognitive Neuropsychology* 3: 1–36.

Snowling, M. (1994) 'Towards a model of spelling acquisition: the development of some component skills', in G. D. A. Brown and N. C. Ellis, *Handbook of Spelling: Theory, Process and Intervention*, Chichester: Wiley.

Snowling, M., Stothard, S. E. and McLean, J. (1996) *The Graded Nonword Reading Test*, Bury St Edmunds: Thames Valley Test Publishing Company.

Stahl, S. A. and Murray, B. A. (1994) 'Defining phonological awareness and its relationship to early reading', *Journal of Educational Psychology* 86: 221–34.

Stainthorp, R. (1994) 'A longitudinal study of the development of reading strategies in 7–11 year old children', unpublished doctoral thesis, London: University of London.

Stainthorp, R. (1997) 'A children's author recognition test: A useful tool in reading research', *Journal of Research in Reading* 20(2): 148–58.

Stainthorp, R. and Hughes, D. (1995) 'Young early readers: a preliminary report of the development of a group of children who were able to read fluently before Key Stage 1', in B. Raban-Bisby, G. Brookes and S. Wolfendale (eds), *Developing Language and Literacy*, Stoke-on-Trent: Trentham Books.

Stainthorp, R. and Hughes, D. (1998) 'Phonological sensitivity and reading: evidence from precocious readers', *Journal of Research in Reading* 21(1): 53–67.

Stanovich, K. E. and West, R. F. (1989) 'Exposure to print and orthographic processing', *Reading Research Quarterly* 24: 400–33.

Stanovich, K. E. (1986) 'Matthew effects in reading: some consequences of individual differences in the acquisition of literacy', *Reading Research Quarterly* 21: 360–407.

Stanovich, K. E. (1992) 'Speculation on the causes and consequences of individual differences in early reading acquisition', in P. B. Gough, L. C. Ehri and

R. Treiman (eds), *Reading Acquisition*, Hillsdale, NJ: Lawrence Erlbaum Associates.

Stuart, M. (1990) 'Processing strategies in a phoneme deletion task', *Quarterly Journal of Experimental Psychology* 42A (2): 305–27.

Stuart, M. (1995) 'Recognizing printed words unlocks the door to reading: how do children find the key?', in E. Funnell and M. Stuart (eds), *Learning to Read*, Oxford: Blackwell.

Stuart, M. and Coltheart, M. (1988) 'Does reading develop in a sequence of stages?', *Cognition* 30: 139–81.

Taylor, J. (1997) 'Trouble with e?', *Handwriting Review* 11: 57–60.

Treiman, R. (1988) 'The internal structure of the syllable', in G. Carlson and M. Tanehaus (eds), *Structure in Language Processing*, Dordrecht (NL): Kluger, pp. 27–52.

Wilde, S. (1996) 'Just periods and exclamation points: the continued development of children's knowledge about punctuation', in N. Hall and A. Robinson (eds), *Learning about Punctuation*, Clevedon: Multilingual Matters.

SUBJECT INDEX

NAME INDEX